Advancing Education for Sustainable Development: A German-Namibian Educator Exchange Program

Barbara Scharfbillig

Gijsbertha van Rooyen

Patricia Ndjavera

Teresa Noichl

FSC
www.fsc.org
MIX
Papier aus ver-
antwortungsvollen
Quellen
Paper from
responsible sources
FSC® C105338

Advancing Education for Sustainable Development: A German-Namibian Educator Exchange Program

Barbara Scharfbillig
Gijsbertha van Rooyen
Patricia Ndjavera
Teresa Noichl

Imprint

© 2025, Suni e.V., Trier, Germany & Gobabis, Namibia
ISBN: 978-3-7583-4265-3

Barbara Scharfbillig, Gijsbertha van Rooyen,
Patricia Ndjavera & Teresa Noichl

Suni e.V.
Clara-Viebig-Str.11
54294 Trier, Germany
www.suni-ev.de
kontakt@suni-ev.de

Light for the Children W.O. 427
Mahahero Steet, Epako,
9000 Gobabis, Namibia
www.lightforthechildren.com
gijsbertha@lightforthechildren.com

Proofreading: Maury Fernandéz Clark, Annika Hoffmann
& Jan Kelkel

Publisher: BoD · Books on Demand GmbH, Überseering 33,
22297 Hamburg, bod@bod.de
Print: Libri Plureos GmbH, Friedensallee 273,
22763 Hamburg

Bibliografische Information der Deutschen Nationalbibliothek: Die Deutsche Nationalbibliothek verzeichnet diese
Publikation in der Deutschen Nationalbibliografie;
detaillierte bibliografische Daten sind im Internet über
dnb.dnb.de abrufbar.

Bibliographical information of the German National
Library: The German National Library lists this publication
in the German National Bibliography;
Detailed bibliographic data is available on the Internet at
dnb.dnb.de.

Index

A note from the authors about "perspective"

This is the second time Suni e.V. and the Light for the Children Foundation organised a two-year exchange program for educators. We, as organisers of the exchange of educators, see our non-profit-organisations as learning organisms, who thrive to be more inclusive, respectful and sensitive to the issues of our members, beneficiaries as well as German and Namibian society. We strive to work with each other on an equal footing, reduce power imbalances and do our best not to reproduce stereotypes. Furthermore, we aim to approach our experiences and contributions with honesty and reflection, endeavouring to embrace all perspectives while remaining sensitive to both German and Namibian cultures.

To this end, we regularly reflect on our experiences, perspectives, biases and work. We do our best to implement the Sustainable Development Goals, follow Human Rights and Children Rights Charta and advocate for better relations between Germany and Namibia by, for example, recognizing the German genocides on the area of Namibia during colonial time.

Additionally, we do our best to make our world a better place. However, a characterisation of this objective as "simple" seems to be far-fetched. Not only do we see conflicts in achieving the SDGs altogether, but we, as organisations, are not divers enough to reflect all perspectives in this document. We are placed in societies with racism, discrimination and imbalances, which sometimes have a normality in day-to-day life and are difficult to identify for ourselves.

Therefore, this document shares the intersubjective perspective of the authors. It is not only based on personal experience, but also on our work as well as commitment and, consequently, reflects our norms, ethics and experiences as personal individuals. As a result, this document may still contain certain imbalances and biases.

Given this circumstance, we highly appreciate every input, every criticism and every insight into a perspective we missed and did not consider. We are willing to learn, to improve and to change our perspective.

Acknowledgements

The exchange of German and Namibian educators, which took place in Germany and Namibia in 2022 and 2023, was supported by many individuals, institutions and organisations:

Educational institutions in Namibia and in Germany opened their doors for the exchange group and gave them an inside into their daily work. We would like to thank the Gobabis Project School in Gobabis, Mokaleng Roman Catholic Combined School in Aminuis, Mokganedi Thlabanello High School in Drimiopsis, Nossob Combined School in Witvlei, catholic day care centre KiTa St. Erasmus in Trassem, catholic day care centre KiTa Rebengarten in Zeltingen, catholic day care centre KiTa St. Martin in Nittel, Keune Primary School in Trier, Free-Montessori-School in Landau, Gobabeb Namib Research Institute and Trier University with its BioGeoLab.

The exchange was, furthermore, supported by volunteers, stakeholders and experts from different fields. In this context, thanks to Alissa Jahn (Suni e.V.), Boiddy Akende Ntesa (Senior Education Officer, Ministry of Education), Christopher Groß (Trier University, Geography and its didactics), Clara Hörmann (African-German Youth Office), Claudia Meurer (Haus der Kleinen Forscher Trier), Claudia Wagner (Suni e.V.), Constance Wantenaar (Directorate of Education at Omaheke Regional Council), Corinna Ernst (Suni e.V.), Corinna Seer (Suni e.V.), Elliot Murangi, Eugen Frisen (Suni e.V.), Eugen Marais (Gobabeb Namib Research Institute), Fiona Mokathu (Suni e.V.), Franz Pauly (Local municipality of Igel), Prof. Dr. Hannes Schmalor (Trier University), Dr. Helene Steigerthal (Suni e.V.), Henk Olwage (Light for the Children Foundation), Julia Frisen (Suni e.V.), Jack-Louis van Rooyen (Light for the Children Foundation), Klaus A. Hess (German-Namibian Society), Klothilde Scharfbillig (Winery Scharfbillig), Lisa Niemann (Suni e.V.), Maren Paulmann (Mosellum Koblenz), Martin Kurzweil (Suni e.V.), Nadine Dolfen (Aids and drug prevention Bergheim), Petra Marker (City library Trier), Hon. Pijoo Nganate (Gouverneur of the Omaheke Region), Rixa Moreno (Engagement Global gGmbH), Sabine Mock (Lokale Agenda 21 Trier), Sebastian Scharfbillig (Winery Scharfbillig), Sebedeus Naibabthe (Ministry of Education), Stephan Scharfbillig sen. (Winery Scharfbillig), Steffanie Knapp (Suni e.V.), Verena Scharfbillig (Winery Scharfbillig), working group on biology didactics and sustainable regional and site development (Trier University) & Vernon Malumani (Suni e.V.).

Special thanks go to Angela Jensen from THE BLUE MIND e.V. for her inspiration, support and ideas as well as to the teams of Gobabeb Namib Research Institute and the Trier University for their training and support. A special thanks also goes to Maury Fernandez Clark (Suni e.V.), Annika Hoffmann (Trier University) and Jan Kelkel (Trier University) for proofreading this report.

Our special thanks to Estellé and Andre Swanepoel for promoting German-Namibian co-operation.

We also would like to thank all German and Namibian sponsors for their donations, their monetary support and their advice: The program was supported by the Directorate of Education Omaheke Regional Council, the Dr. Buhmann Stiftung, the Rhineland-Palatinate Development Policy Network ELAN e.V., the German-Namibian Society DNG e.V., the Catholic Fonds, the Light for the Children Foundation, the Sparkasse Trier, the German-Namibian Society, Trier University and the Office of the Governor in Omaheke Region. The exchange was financed 75% by the German-African Youth Office (AGYO) with Engagement Global gGmbH on behalf of the German Federal Ministry for Economic Cooperation and Development. Thanks to the AGYO and their amazing team of project managers, project coordinators and financial advisors.

Lastly, we would like to thank the participants and group leaders of the German-Namibian exchange of educators. Without their enthusiasm, thrive and open minds, this project would have not been successful. This publication contains personal in-sights into the experiences of the participants, which is why their names are not mentioned here. Nevertheless, our deepest thanks go to them.

Index of abbreviations

AGYO	African-German Youth Office
EE	Environmental Education
ENSA	Entwicklungspolitisches Schulaustauschprogramm (Development policy school exchange program)
ESD	Education for Sustainable Development
LftC	Light for the Children Foundation
NEEN	Namibian Environmental Education Network
NPO	Non-Profit-Organisation
SDG	Sustainable Development Goal
UN	United Nations

List of illustrations

Photo: Trier, 2022, Suni e.V.

1. Introduction

Over a period of two years, the German-Namibian non-profit organisation (NPO) Suni e.V., in collaboration with the Namibian NPO Light for the Children Foundation W.O. 427 and the Directorate of Education at the Omaheke Regional Council in Gobabis, facilitated a German-Namibian exchange of educators. This project aimed to equip educators from both countries with enhanced knowledge, intercultural competencies, and training in Education for Sustainable Development (ESD), thereby empowering them to act as catalysts for societal change.

Fourteen highly motivated educators from diverse educational fields participated in the exchange, which featured ten workshops, numerous webinars, two study tours, and an international project collaboration. Participants travelled between both countries, gaining insights into each other's educational practices. They completed ESD training at Trier University in Germany and the Gobabeb Namib Research Institute in Namibia. Working in three German-Namibian project teams, they developed and published educational modules on deforestation, water filtration, and water pollution, ultimately reaching over 200 children in Germany and Namibia. These learning modules are also accessible online for wider use.

Throughout the project, participants faced several challenges, left their comfort zones, and engaged in introspective exploration. They grew into a cohesive German-Namibian team, embracing new perspectives, expanding their horizons, and gaining invaluable insights into each other's educational systems and cultures. By the project's conclusion, they not only met but exceeded the expectations set for this exchange format. However, the journey was not without difficulties; all parties made mistakes, engaged in open communication, and learned from these experiences, deepening their mutual understanding.

When Suni e.V. and the Light for the Children Foundation initiated this endeavour in 2015, there was scarce published material and insights from other NPOs or experts were greatly needed. Consequently, They have chosen to document their experiences to foster transparency.

This publication aims to provide an in-depth look into the organisation, implementation, and outcomes of the German-Namibian exchange. It begins by detailing each step of the planning process and offering comprehensive information on the varied aspects to consider when arranging an international exchange program between Germany and Namibia.

Following this, the document outlines the implementation processes and includes schedules of different segments of the exchange. The NPOs candidly address their mistakes and share the lessons learned to guide others in avoiding similar pitfalls. This report provides an overview of the ESD project work conducted in international teams and discusses their experiences facilitating such projects. After describing the monitoring and evaluation process, the authors examine various outcome levels, analysing both intended and unforeseen results within a broader context. The document concludes with recommendations on which elements of the exchange program could be retained and which could be improved.

By sharing their experiences in detail, Suni e.V. and Light for the Children Foundation hope others can learn from their mistakes, identify best practices, and adapt the insights gained to their projects when applicable. While the authors aim for objectivity, this document reflects personal experiences and the societal norms and values in which they are embedded. Consequently, it may contain certain imbalances and biases.

2. Concept and planning of a Namibian-German exchange in the context of Education for Sustainable Development

From March 2021 to December 2022, Light for the Children Foundation (LftC) and Suni e.V. conducted an exchange program between Namibian and German educators, including ten workshops in Namibia and Germany, several webinars and online sessions, a study tour with a training in Germany and another one with a training in Namibia. The objective of the program was to implement the Sustainable Development Goal (SDG) number four "Ensure inclusive and equitable quality education and promote lifelong learning opportunities for all"[1] and the SDG No. 17 "Strengthen the means of implementation and revitalize the global partnership for sustainable development"[2]. Additionally, the focus of the exchange was on the SDG indicator 4.7. "Ensure all learners acquire knowledge and skills needed to promote sustainable development, including among others through Education for Sustainable Development and sustainable lifestyles, human rights, gender equality, promotion of a culture of peace and non-violence, global citizenship, and appreciation of cultural diversity and of culture's contribution to sustainable development"[3].

Fourteen Namibian and German educators were trained in the field of Education for Sustainable Development. They worked together for two years and implemented educational projects related to SDG 4.7. In this chapter, the partner-institutions of the exchange will be introduced, and the planning process will be explained. Crucial aspects such as diversity, finances and the selection of candidates will be addressed and solutions for potential problems during the planning process will be identified.

2.1 The partner organisations of the exchange

The Light for the Children Foundation W.O. 427 is a registered non-profit organisation in Namibia. The Foundation started off organically, inside a financially disadvantaged community in Gobabis in 1999. Its main contributors are community members dedicated to caregiving, teaching and leading and aims to comprehensively serve orphans and vulnerable children while developing a vision for their future. Light for the Children Foundation's main centre is located in the city of Gobabis in Namibia. Daily, more than 300 children come for education, attention, health care and food. They are being helped at every phase of their growth, from toddlers to young adults. Nevertheless, in collaboration with its partner project, Steps for Children, training is also offered to adults. The purpose of the Foundation is to ensure that every child, no matter how unfavourable their circumstances, may have a clear vision for the future and a firm foundation in life. LftC runs an outreach program in Omaheke Region and facilitates the Lighthouse, a short-term foster care centre for children, who need immediate help with the only baby hatch in the region. The LftC trains its staff regularly and runs a volunteer program for young people from Germany and the Netherlands. It has 32 employees in Gobabis.

Suni e.V. is a multinational non-profit organisation that is based in Germany. It operates in Namibia and in Germany and embarks to fulfil the United Nations Sustainable Development Goals, particularly the goal number four. It supports vulnerable children and young adults in the Omaheke region in Namibia and fosters intercultural exchange between Germans and Namibians. Suni e.V. sustainably improves educational opportunities and living standards at educational institutions through intercultural exchanges, transfer of knowledge and financial support. It has organised study tours to Germany for Namibian teachers and vice versa. Suni e.V. is a certified place of Education for Sustainable Development in the German states of Rhineland-Palatinate and Saarland. It has signed the Initiative Transparent Civil Society in Germany. It is a member of the German-Namibian Society and the Development Network of the German state of Rhineland-Palatinate. Suni e.V. is a volunteer based NPO with 130 members.

Suni e.V. and the Light for the Children Foundation have been in official partnership since 2016 but have been in contact since 2011. Both NPOs put forward a delegate to design and coordinate the exchange project - who were employed in both countries. Additionally, both NPOs had volunteers contributing to the implementation of the exchange project. Before implementing the exchange, both NPOs teamed up with the Directorate of Education in Gobabis Directorate of Education at Omaheke Regional Council in Gobabis. As the supervisory authority, the directorate gave their approval and took over the transport in Namibia.

The two NPOs were supported by many other organisations and educational institutions in Germany and Namibia, who opened their doors for the exchange group. Partners in the field of Education for Sustainable Development were the Gobabeb Namib Research Institute, who implemented the ESD training of the exchange group in the Namib Desert in Namibia. In Germany, THE BLUE MIND e.V. and employees of the biology and its didactics at Trier University took over the ESD training.

2.2 Overall topic: Education for Sustainable Development

ESD is anchored in the Sustainable Development Goals of the Agenda 2030, a worldwide action plan to address numerous problems of our planet and to achieve a prosperous life for all people on Earth. Subgoal 4.7 says that all learners on this planet should "[…] acquire the knowledge and skills needed to promote sustainable development, including, among others, through education for sustainable development and sustainable lifestyles, human rights, gender equality, promotion of a culture of peace and non-violence, global citizenship and appreciation of cultural diversity and of culture's contribution to sustainable development"[4]. ESD gives learners this knowledge, skills, values and agency to address interconnected global challenges including climate change, loss of biodiversity, unsustainable use of resources and inequality. It empowers learners of all ages to make informed decisions and take individual and collective action to change society and care for the planet to fulfil the SDGs. ESD is based on four fundamental pillars of sustainable development: social, economic, environmental and political. Implementing sustainability is seen as a lifelong learning process and an integral part of quality education worldwide. Therefore, ESD is one of the most developing areas in education, and it was chosen to be not only the topic of the exchange, but woven into all areas of the exchange format.

2.2.1 ESD in Germany and Rhineland-Palatinate

Germany has a national action plan on Education for Sustainable Development[5]. The fields of action, goals and measures are structured according to the central educational areas of early childhood education, school, vocational training, higher education and formal and informal learning. The specific recommendations outlined in the action plan aim to ensure that ESD is firmly embedded within the various sectors of the German educational landscape. However, since every state in Germany has its own educational system, the implementation of the action plan differs from state to state.

In 2020, the SDGs were anchored in Section 1 of the Rhineland-Palatinate School Act[6] and in the state sustainability strategy[7]. A quality management and certification system for out-of-school education providers was introduced with the federal state of Saarland. In Rhineland-Palatinate, there are at least 93 extracurricular ESD learning sites[8] as well as a wide range of educational institutions of all kinds that are certified as ESD schools or ESD educational institutions. Over 80 schools are organised in the Network Education for Sustainable Development Rhineland-Palatinate[9]. For educators at daycare centres, there is only one ESD continuing education program in the state[10]. Teachers on the other hand have a variety of education opportunities around ESD[11] and student teachers have a diverse range of ESD courses and ESD projects at the various universities in Rhineland-Palatinate. Germany in general and the state of Rhineland-Palatinate in particular offers the exchange program on a wide variety of possible learning sites for ESD.

2.2.2 ESD in Namibia and Omaheke Region

The Namibian National Environmental Education and Education for Sustainable Development Policy[12], instituted in 2019 as a "first of its kind in Southern Africa, highlights training and capacity building in ESD as one of the main strategies for addressing sustainable development challenges [...]"[13] and working towards the SDGs. Environmental Education (EE) and ESD are recognized as "[...] one of the means of realizing the dynamic balance among environmental factors and socio-economic advancement and accelerating progress towards sustainable development"[14]. ESD in Namibia is mainly intertwined with Environmental Education, although the other dimensions of ESD are not absent. Namibia has established a Namibian Environmental Education Network (NEEN) with educational institutions around the country, functioning as an umbrella organisation and a networking platform.

The University of Namibia and other Namibian universities offer EE and ESD projects for teachers under the name Change Projects[15]. Further training in ESD for educators is offered by various NPOs such as the Namib Desert Environmental Education Trust (NaDEET)[16] and the Gobabeb Research and Training Center[17] - most of them focus on EE. Currently, there are no certification bodies for ESD learning sites or educational institutions.

In Omaheke Region, no ESD learning facility existed, but two schools were part of NEEN. Therefore, the possibility of getting expert partners in Omaheke was limited, and LftC found partners in the field of ESD in other Namibian Regions.

2.2.3 SDGs and ESD in the exchange

Suni e.V. was in the process of certifying as a place of ESD when the exchange project started and has been certified as an ESD learning site in Rhineland-Palatinate and Saarland since May 2023. To increase its own expertise in the field of ESD, Suni e.V. joined forces during the exchange project with experts from THE BLUE MIND e.V. and Trier University. Additionally, several ESD learning sites and ESD experts have been consulted, such as Haus der kleinen Forscher, Mosellum, Lokale Agenda 21 Trier and the experts of the promoter program of the Rhineland-Palatinate development policy network. The Light for the Children Foundation implemented the ESD training with the Gobabeb Namib Research Institute and Training Center[18] in Erongo Region.

ESD and the implementation of the SDGs during the exchange proved to be challenging for the two NPOs: The 2030 Agenda emphasizes the need to live in a world in which humanity lives in harmony with nature. Global

warming is to be stopped, nature conservation is firmly anchored and an awareness of sustainable lifestyles is part of the implementation of the SDGs as ESD. At the same time, the SDGs are based on a global economic system with whose underlying prosperity and growth model the so-called more developed countries have led the world community into the environmental and resource crisis. SDG 8 calls for growth in annual gross domestic product, while studies clearly show that this is not compatible with other SDGs[19]. The commitment to permanent economic growth worldwide is at odds with the planetary boundaries that are to be protected.

There were also discrepancies in the planning and implementation of the exchange project. On the one hand, criteria of eco-social procurement were emphasized in all areas and the implementation of the SDGs was considered in detail. The consumption of drinking water in Germany, regional catering in general, the use of second-hand material for the workshops and the planting of trees as a group activity are some examples how sustainability was considered. On the other hand, all participants caused a lot of environmental pollution by travelling between Namibia and Germany. The massive consumption of resources by the participants was at odds with the sustainable lifestyle that was to be communicated. In the conception, the organisers decided to argue that the negative ecological *footprint*[20] of the participants was justified because of the ecological *handprint*[21] and the fact that the participants would spread ESD as multipliers and become socially or politically active. Chapter 8 provides a conclusion on whether this argument holds up against the facts.

"The implementation of the SDGs during the exchange proved to be challenging for the two NPOs."

Suni e.V. & Light for the Children Foundation

2.3 Framework and planning process

Suni e.V. and the Light for the Children Foundation had implemented an exchange program with the funding program "weltwärts exchange projects - Global partnerships for the Agenda 2030"[22] before the Corona Pandemic. The impact exceeded expectations, leading both NPOs to plan a repeat of the exchange. They intended to apply for the same funding line when the Corona pandemic began. They waited until 2020 when travel restrictions were lifted to apply at the newly founded African-German Youth Office (AGYO) with Engagement Global gGmbH. The topic of Education for Sustainable Development was chosen by a vocal group of educators from the previous exchange, because both NPOs are working in the field of education and the teaching of ESD had become more important in both countries. Due to Suni e.V. based in the German state of Rhineland-Palatinate and the LftCF in Namibia's Omaheke Region, it was decided to implement the project in the spatial borders of Rhineland-Palatinate and Omaheke Region only.

The partner NPOs determined the number of participants based on capacity. The legal framework and timing were mainly set by the funding program *Teams up!* due to the fact that the AGYO was funding 75% of the project's expenses. Therefore, the participants should not be older than 30 years. The writing of applications took up a lot of time and was carried out mainly in Germany.

The content of the training courses in the field of ESD was not finalized until May 2022 for the training in Germany and March 2023 for the training in Namibia. In March 2021, the German-Namibian exchange of educators started officially. The program ended in December 2022.

2.4 Aims

Overall, the exchange aimed at addressing the SDG 4.c. "By 2030, substantially increase the supply of qualified teachers, including through international cooperation for teacher training in developing countries, especially least developed countries and small island developing States.[23]"and SDG 4.7. "By 2030, ensure that all learners acquire the knowledge and skills needed to promote sustainable development[…][24]". The exchange was designed to enable participants to become multipliers for Education for Sustainable Development (ESD) in Namibia and Germany, teaching children about sustainable lifestyles.

On a personal level, educators should enhance their intercultural competencies, challenge the own stereotypes, acquire new knowledge, learn innovative methods, build connections and ultimately shift their perspectives.

2.5 Inclusion, diversity and gender issues

When planning the exchange, the "Diversity in Youth Exchange Checklist" by Magdalena Zatylna and Dominik Mosiczuk[25] from the German-Polish Youth Office was utilized to ensure that the program promotes diversity.

Additionally, there were specific circumstances that were considered by the organisers: Being a parent or becoming pregnant during the exchange was one of them. Specific measurements were put in place to make sure that parents and pregnant women could participate. Part of these measurements was awareness: It was communicated that being a parent is a special challenge when travelling as part of an exchange program, and that the coordinators would support any parent and any becoming parent individually. For instance, parents were permitted to bring their young children to the workshops. Furthermore, the entire group was encouraged to support one another and assist parents when children needed to be brought along. Several participants from Namibia were parents, one participant gave birth before the first encounter and one during the program. However, no participant had to drop out and, consequently, the measurements seemed to have been successful.

A second field of consideration was gender: In both countries, there is a gender imbalance in the educational field, with more women than other genders working in this area. The selection of the participants reflected this circumstance. The different cultural and religious rules concerning sleeping arrangements and genders were considered when booking accommodation. Also, specific cultural roles of genders and age groups were discussed and respected in the planning phase. Participants also discussed the topic of gender within the preparation.

For the purpose of ensuring that participants of all financial backgrounds could take part in the exchange, the program was almost fully financed for them. In this context, the coordinators maintained open communication with participants identified as having limited financial resources and provided assistance twice during the exchange to guarantee they could remain in the program.

Participants with learning disabilities, special needs and physical limitations were proactively invited to apply for the exchange, but, however, no such individuals were identified. Furthermore, to avoid accusations of tribalism within the Namibian context, careful attention was given to ensuring a heterogeneous composition of language and cultural groups in the Namibian contingent.

2.6 Schedule of the exchange program

To plan the exchange program, a detailed Gantt chart was used to identify milestones, timeframes and parallel operations. The primary risk identified during the planning phase was the potential rejection of visa applications for the Namibian educators. The two study tours to Germany and Namibia were the main milestones of the program. The third milestone was the implementation of partner projects between a German and a Namibian educator.

Despite the previously mentioned aspects, it was essential to take into account the Namibian school holidays as well as those of three federal states in Germany.

2.7 Finances and funding

The program budget included accommodation, catering, travel costs, fees and royalties, material and equipment, costs for group building activities, rent, visa fees, insurance, administration costs, project costs and salaries.

Managing finances was a challenge, because the organisers received over one thousand receipts over the course of the two-year period. However, with a shared online document and regular online meetings, the administration was made possible. The final financial itinerary was put in place by the German NPO. The two coordinators were supported by two additional heads of finances from the two partner NPOs.

In Namibia, getting receipts from informal taxi drivers proved to be a challenge. That is why Namibian participants always travelled with a receipt pad. Whenever it was foreseen that the group would provide itself with food, participants managed small amounts on their own. The group leaders prepared a statement of account. To ensure the Namibian NPO had sufficient funds for the program, the German NPO transferred the necessary amount, if possible, in advance, but there were deficits.

The entire exchange project received 75% of its funding from the AGYO at Engagement Global, sourced from the German Federal Ministry for Economic Cooperation and Development. Co-sponsors were the Entwicklungspolitisches Landesnetzwerk Rheinland-Pfalz, the Sparkasse Trier, the German-Namibian Society, the Buhmann Foundation, the Directorate of Education Omaheke Regional Council as well as Suni e.V. and the Light for the Children Foundation.

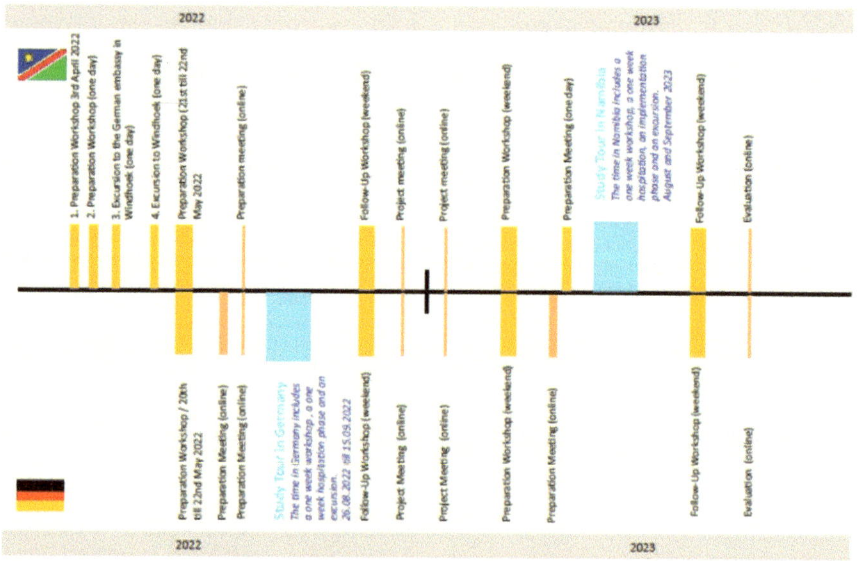

Figure 1: Simplified version of the schedule of the German-Namibian exchange of educators, 2022, Suni e.V.

Overview of cost items	
Accommodation	Hotels and Backpackers in Germany and Namibia for the preparation workshops, follow-up workshops, as well as for the exchange itself
Catering	Food and drinks in Germany and in Namibia
Transport	Travel costs for the workshops, flights to Germany and Namibia, travel costs to the airport and for the Namibians to the German embassy in Windhoek for visa interviews
Royalties	Entrance fees and royalties for lectures
Material	Equipment for the workshops, all costs related to the participant's-projects
Rent	Rent for rooms to hold workshops, rent for an office
Visa Fees	Visa fees for the Namibians, all other costs related to visa documentation and the interview at the German embassy in Windhoek
Insurance	Health and travel insurance, insurances of the organisations
Administrations costs	Copies, paper, ink, telephone charges, office material and other items related to administration
Salaries	Salary for two coordinators, allowances for the group leaders
Other costs	costs for group building activities

Figure 2: Tabular overview of the cost items incurred in the exchange program, 2022, Suni e.V.

Additional support was given by several individual lecturers and experts who waived a fee.

The fundraising process started nine months prior to the beginning of the two-year exchange program. The process continued until the beginning of the second year. There were no participation fees.

2.8 Selecting participants and group leaders

The exchange program was designed for fourteen educators, with potential participants required to apply for inclusion. They were selected after an online interview with the national coordinator and sometimes together with both coordinators. In contrast to Germany, there were significantly more applicants from Namibia.

In Namibia, seven educators with different home languages[26] and backgrounds, all from the Omaheke Region, were selected. In comparison, in Germany, all seven participants were German-speaking female educators with different academic backgrounds. The economic status of the participants varied greatly as well. The participants included students in the field of education, early childhood educators, primary and secondary school teachers, a relief teacher, a scientific employee of a university as well as an employee of the Ministry of Education. In Germany, all participants, organisers and group leaders were women, because no men applied for any position. Due to the AGYO guidelines, all applicants were 30 or younger at the time of the project. Both NPOs were criticised by school

officials and interested individuals several times for this age limit and there was a total of 13 responses expressing a desire to raise the age limit.

Each group in Namibia and Germany had one group leader. The Namibian group leader had experience working with German volunteers in Namibia, had been to Germany several times, and was a group leader of an exchange project before. The German group leader had been to Namibia before. They fulfilled the role of group speakers and counsellors and took over administrative tasks. They were part of the group and are therefore included when talking about participants in this document.

Photo 1: Namibian group, Gobabis, 2022, LftC
Photo 2: German group, Trier, 2022, Suni e.V.

3. Preparation for the exchange program

To prepare all participants for their trips and projects, a series of workshops, webinars, and online meetings were conducted. In Namibia, these workshops and meetings were held in Gobabis, as it was easily accessible for all participants. In Germany, the sessions took place in Rhineland-Palatinate, specifically in Trier and Gunderath. Initially, only the first workshops were held at different dates in both countries. The reason for the time difference was that in Namibia, the preparation took two months longer because the complex procurement of visas had to be considered. However, all subsequent workshops were held simultaneously, allowing participants to exchange ideas and support one another. In addition to the group sessions, each participant also engaged in individual preparation.

3.1 Preparation for the Namibian group

The preparation in Namibia included two one-day workshops, one excursion to Windhoek and a two-day workshop. The first workshop only covered the issue of visa application and the introduction of the partner NPO. The second and third workshops included general information about Germany (history, geography, train system), the German education system, culture shock, stereotypes, health restrictions and the SDGs. The trip to Windhoek was undertaken for visa interviews at the German embassy in Namibia. In addition to the workshops, the Namibian participants stayed in touch, supported each other with the visa applications and formed groups on social networks.

3.1.1 Visa for the Namibians

The visa requirements for the Namibians could be found on the German embassy website in Namibia (windhuk.diplo.de). Initial pieces of information about the visa application process had already been given to the seven Namibian participants in the first workshop, six months prior to departure. The visa application process in Namibia was overseen by a

The following literature helped the two NPOs to plan the preparation and follow-up workshops as well as online activities during the two exchange tours:

Adrianna Babjiew a.o. (2014). Eurogames, Games and exercises for international youth exchange.

IJAB – Fachstelle für Internationale Jugendarbeit der Bundesrepublik Deutschland e. V. (2021). Virtuelle Internationale Jugendbegegnungen organisieren.

Klub Klise (2014). Methods Collection, International youth exchange - let`s learn from each other.

Ludovic Fresse & Ines Grau (2015). Geschichte und Erinnerung in internationalen Jugendbegegnungen

Terry Heick (2017). 15 Reflection Strategies To Help Students Retain What You Just Taught Them.

Vernon Malumani, Patricia Ndjavera, Gijsbertha van Rooyen & Barbara Scharfbillig (2017). Organising a Namibian-German exchange of Educators.

Owen Ginzburg (2004). The Hungry Man.

Owen Ginzburg (2005). There you go!

Gilberte Raymond Driesen (2016). Help expresses a balance of power. Interview with former teacher Gilberte Raymonde Driesen about colonial behaviour in school partnership

glokal e.V. (2016). Mit kolonialen Grüßen...

glokal e.V. (2016). Das Märchen von der Augenhöhe.

Berliner Entwicklungspolitischer Ratschlag (2013). Develop-mental Turn.

consultant agency and not by the embassy itself. The documents to be submitted included the application form, confirmation of employment, bank statements, invitation letters, flight tickets, health insurance, schedule of the study tour, other personal documents and confirmation letters. As already mentioned, the Namibian participants had to visit the agency in Windhoek for a personal interview. After the interview, some Namibians were asked to submit additional documents due to loss of documents or due to not making a copy at the agency. After some huzzle, the coordinators got in contact with the embassy directly. In the end, the visas were granted several weeks prior to departure. The visa application process was supported by the Namibian travel company EXPERT TRAVEL CC.

3.1.2 Insurance and health

All Namibian participants received a health insurance, which was valid in the Schengen countries of the European Union. The insurance provider was Hollard Insurance Company in Namibia. They also had a group insurance with the German NPO. This meant that if they became sick, they were required to pay for their treatment upfront and subsequently seek reimbursement from their insurance. Some Namibians got sick during their time in Germany, but none had to visit a doctor's office. All Namibians had to have valid vaccinations against the coronavirus, but no other vaccination was necessary for the purpose of travelling to Germany.

For a pregnant participant, a personal contact with a midwife was established during the initial days of their encounter in Germany, ensuring she had a professional to consult if any issues arose.

3.1.3 Cultures and languages of Germany

Germans, who had been working or living in Namibia, and a Namibian, who lived in Germany, taught the Namibian group different aspects of Germany, such as the political system, history, geography and cultural aspects. Additionally, each participant had contact to a Namibian colleague, who had travelled to Germany before, and they prepared themselves individually. Due to the educators full-time jobs and other commitments, learning German was not an objective of the preparation.

3.1.4 Other topics

The behaviour and expectations of a guest staying with a host vary between Namibia and Germany. Consequently, both the German and Namibians prepared a list of topics to discuss with their respective guests or hosts before the first study tour started.

This list covered food, the host's family and living conditions, money, expectations, personal hygiene and sleeping arrangements.

Besides food and accommodation, participants were, furthermore, informed that money was needed for the trip to Germany. Namibian participants were given the opportunity to create a savings plan with the Namibian coordinator. This offer was used. Nevertheless, financial problems arose.

Social media usage varies between Germany and Namibia. It was important to inform the Namibian participants about the German legal restrictions concerning posting photos of others, especially children, on one's own social media account.

3.2 Preparation for the German group

The preparation in Germany was held in a three-day workshop. After the study tour in Germany, two more workshops were held – one for the reflection on the Namibians visit and one workshop dedicated exclusively to preparing for the trip to Namibia. The German group had more time (more than a year) to prepare for their visit to Namibia. The workshops covered general topics on Namibia (history, geography, climate, languages), health, culture shock and other topics. The Germans received a travel guide for Namibia and additional literature about Namibia.

Literature about Germany:

Get the free travel guide:
Facts about Germany
www.tatsachen-ueber-deutschland.de/en

A good site to learn more about Germany is
www.deutschland.de/en

Free App to learn German
www.memrise.com

3.2.1 Visa for the Germans

The German participants only had to fill out the visa form at the Namibian border checkpoint at Hosea Kutako International Airport on arrival in Namibia. They had to fill in the address and phone number of their first accommodation.

3.2.2 Insurance and health in Namibia

The German participants had their own health insurance, travel insurance, accident insurance and indemnity insurance. In one of the workshops, a German nurse and AIDS-educator with experience living in Namibia was invited to address questions regarding immunisations, travel sicknesses and common health problems for Germans travelling to Namibia. She also discussed HIV and AIDS with the participants, highlighting that AIDS is the leading cause of death in Namibia and that approximately one in ten Namibians is living with HIV[27].

3.2.3 Cultures and languages of Namibia

According to the Namibian Constitution, there are thirteen national languages. Eight of them are spoken in Omaheke Region: Afrikaans, English, Ju/hoansi, Khoekhoegowab, Otjiherero, Oshiwambo, RuKwangali and Setswana. To make sure the German participants were as prepared as possible, the Namibians informed them about their home languages and cultural rules. The German participants were encouraged to learn basic phrases in their partner's language and familiarize themselves with essential cultural norms. It should be noted that language animation was not included in this exchange. Namibian English and British English are not the same. For this reason, the whole group had a webinar with a lecturer from the University of Bayreuth on Namibian English(es). Non-verbal communication was part of the preparation.

During the preparation phase, it became clear that at least two members of the German group lacked sufficient English knowledge to conduct a professional conversation. They received special support from the organisers during the exchange and received additional homework to improve their English. The group supported these participants as well. Nonetheless, this posed challenges for the group dynamic, as these participants were often unable to fully engage in discussions or lectures due to their limited language skills.

Although both participants made a huge growth in their language development, proper English language skills would have been beneficiary from the start.

3.2.4 Other preparation

Nights in Namibia are cold during the winter, and heating was not provided in the hosts' accommodation. German participants were therefore especially warned about the climate and advised to pack with the climate in mind.

3.3 Mutual preparation

In addition to the country-specific preparation, the topics of culture and culture shock, stereotypes and racism, the SDGs, child protection and the common colonial history in both country groups were dealt with in the preparation. Additionally, significant emphasis was placed on communication to ensure that existing barriers could be identified and overcome.

Literature about Namibia:

Henning Melber (2014). Understanding Namibia

John Mendelsohn (2010). Atlas of Namibia: A Portrait of the Land and its People

Marion Wallace (2004). History of Namibia: From the Beginning to 1990

Namibia Statistics Agency (2011a). Namibia 2011 Population & Housing Census Main Report

Namibia Statistics Agency (2011b). Namibia 2011 Census Atlas

Peter Pack and Livia Pack (2016). Stefan Loose Reiseführer Namibia

Literature about Namibian languages:

Nduvaa Erna Nguaiko (2010). The New Otjiherero Dictionary

Petrus Angula Mbenzi (2015). Otjiherero Common Expressions and Phrases Beauty Bogwasi und Hannelore

Vögele (2017). Reise Know-How Sprachführer Setswana - Wort für Wort

Esther Ndengu und Gabriel Ndengu (2017). Reise Know-How Sprachführer Oshiwambo - Wort für Wort

Thomas Suelmann (2015). Reise Know-How Sprachführer Afrikaans - Wort für Wort

3.3.1 Culture and Culture Shock

During preparation, all participants were given a presentation by a lecturer about culture shock and reverse culture shock to prepare them for their trips and their return home.

3.3.2 Stereotypes, racism and power relations

Stereotypes are not simply overcome by contact. It is important to analyse the way stereotypes work, the difference between racism, stereotypes and discrimination and why power relations play an important role in people's behaviour. Both countries share a history of systematic racism and genocide. This history was discussed in the preparation meetings. In both groups, the topics of stereotypes, racisms and power relations were reflected, but a different approach was used in Namibia and in Germany:

The German group had a workshop on stereotypes, stigmata and racism with a lecturer from the German NPO ebasa e.V., Ebasa e.V. combines ethnological

"Watch the TED Talk `The danger of a single story´ by Chimamanda Ngozi Adichie."

competence and cultural sensitivity and advises development cooperations. One of the methods to make biases aware was the discussion of the TED-Talk "The danger of a single story" by Chimamanda Ngozi Adichie.

"Language and images can either divide and make stereotypical descriptions – or unify, clarify and create nuanced descriptions of the complex world we live in. For visitors, it can be difficult to present other people and the surroundings accurately in a brief social media post."[28] Therefore, before their travel to Namibia, the German group discussed RadiAid's Social Media Guide for volunteers and travellers as well as colonial continuities, critical whiteness and the white saviour complex.

In Namibia, the participants also discussed the topic of stereotypes, stigma and racisms, since all three are still visible in Namibia. Everyone was able to relate and had examples or experiences to share. The group also spoke about how to avoid stigmatisation and build

towards unity in a diverse culture. Since Omaheke is a highly diverse region, this is a topic, which was relevant to all the participants and something they dealt with every day.

3.3.3 The Sustainable Development Goals

Both groups had the "World's largest lesson"[29] to give them a first introduction into the SDGs before the first encounter. There was a one-day training on the SDGs exclusively in Germany and a refreshing training in Namibia , when the whole group had their ESD training. The participants worked with specific SDGs during their ESD projects. There was no specific preparation on ESD, because this was part of the actual trainings in Germany and Namibia.

3.3.4 Child Care Protection

Since the two organising NPOs are both active in the field of child and youth work and all participants were educators, both groups received training in child protection. All participants were introduced to the child protection policy of Suni e.V. In retrospect, we should have made child protection a topic of discussion. Although the legal situation in both countries was not significantly different, the perspectives on it were very diverse and this topic proved to be controversial in the further course of the exchange.

3.3.5 Talking about the elephant in the room: The mutual colonial history

The genocides in what is now Namibia were part of a campaign of racial extermination and collective punishment by the German Empire against the Ovaherero, Mbanderu, Nama, Damara, San and other groups. The Herero genocide is considered the first genocide of the 20th century, and took place between 1904 and 1908. Since 2015, the Namibian and German governments have been negotiating how to overcome this dark past and how to forge a mutual path in the future. Unfortunately, these negotiations have not been successful so far. Germany has yet to fully confront its brutal colonial past and there is a significant lack of public awareness regarding the lasting impact of colonial crimes, which are still felt in Namibia today. In both groups, the German-Namibian history was part of their preparation, but the coordinators placed special emphasis on the German group's knowledge of colonial history and awareness. They took part in a learning module on German-Namibian colonial history organised by the Suni e.V. association, and they were asked to watch and discuss films about the German-Namibian history and prepare individually.

In Namibia the whole group had a meeting with Mr. Elliot Murangi, secondary teacher in history, geography and Afrikaans and part of the Mbanderu Traditional Authority. He shared a lot of information about the genocide on Herero and Mbanderu people. It was a very open conversation and there was time to ask questions. Overall, the conversation has shed greater light on Namibian history and its enduring consequences.

Other parts of Namibian-German history are of interest too. For example, the personal stories of over 400 men and women in Namibia today, who were child refugees for years in the German Democratic Republic (Eastern Germany) during Namibia's struggle for independence, was another striking aspect of the history in focus

3.4 Communication within a German-Namibian team

Communication with each other is crucial when implementing an exchange program over a long period of time. At the beginning of the project, the NPOs made sure that all participants had access to a smartphone and were connected to each other over at least one online platform or app. Some Namibian participants lacked a stable mobile connection and could therefore not permanently use their phones to participate in online based communication. Nevertheless, they were able to follow along with a delay. This connection was permanent over a two-year period. The coordinators from Germany and Namibia mainly used Zoom, email, WhatsApp and Dropbox to share documents and information. Data protection laws were considered carefully. Communication between coordinators was almost every week. Two personal meetings between the NPO took place over the course of the program. Since there was no budget for meetings between the NPOs, they took place whenever a member of one NPO was in Europe or southern Africa.

During the encounters, the Namibian participants benefited from free Wi-Fi network in Trier. The German participants bought a valid SIM card on arrival in Namibia and had mobile connection during most of their stay.

Mutual communication was done in English, though none of the participants or coordinators spoke English as mother tongue. There was no specific language training, neither for German nor for one of the 13 Namibian national languages, but basic information about phrases and cultural specifics of communication were given at the preparation workshops. Non-verbal communication, such as hand gestures, were considered during the cultural preparation. Additionally, the overall group had a webinar about Namibian English(es) and its special features.

On the third day of the initial encounter, all participants collaboratively developed a set of communication guidelines that everyone agreed to follow throughout the exchange.

The coordinators established a solid communication with all participants, calling them at least once per year for a personal conversation about their wellbeing and keeping up a vivid chat with all participants.

Photo: Workshop about communication, Igel, 2022, Suni e.V.

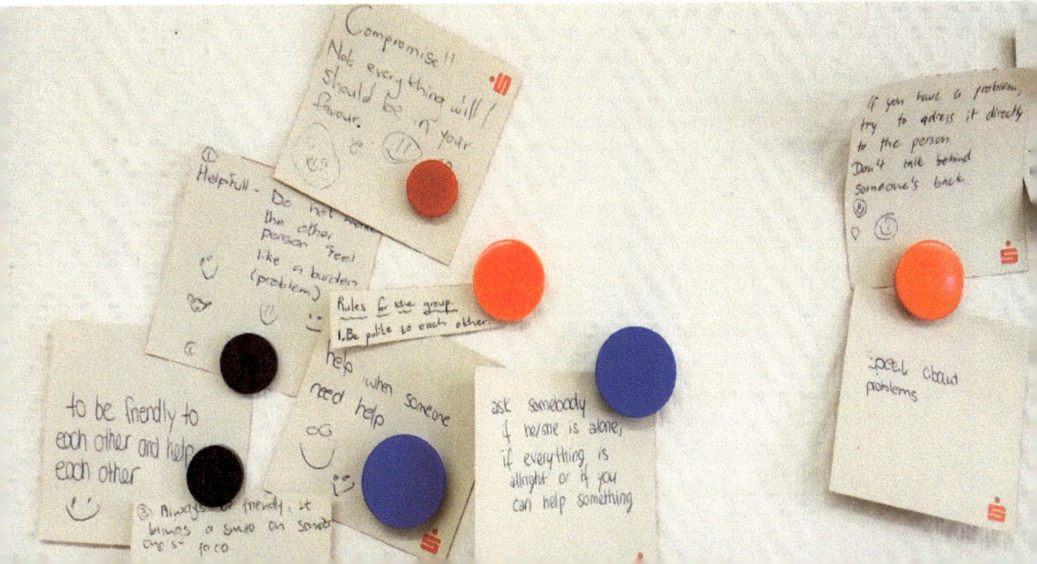

The Namibians also completed a personal behaviour test to get more insight into their own way of thinking and doing. This personality and behavioural test, helped them a lot to increase the understanding of why they act like they used to or why they struggle with something specific. The results of the test provided participants with insights into areas where they could adjust their communication or behaviour to become better team players.

3.5 Legal restrictions in Namibia and in Germany

Germany and Namibia are stable states with a functioning administration, judiciary and police force. Nevertheless, there are differences in the legal restrictions of both countries. The areas of child protection, data protection and traffic regulations were most relevant to the exchange.

Namibia as well as Germany have ratified the Children's Rights Charta, because of which child abuse is punishable. In Germany, Child protection is embedded in the Federal Child Protection Act[30]. Namibia is following the Child Care Protection Act from 2015[31] to give effect to the rights of children. Children's Rights are contained in the Namibian Constitution. Corporal punishment is against the law[32] and prohibited in schools under the Namibian Educational Code of Conduct. The Supreme Court judged in 1991 that the guarantee of human dignity in article 8 of the Constitution[33] precludes the use of corporal punishment in schools. The practical implementation of those similar laws differ in both countries. Corporal punishment in a school context is reported regularly in Namibia.

Germany has high standards for data-protection and privacy laws. Namibia is not having a data-protection act at all. However, various sector-specific laws are in place to protect client information, including the legal and banking sectors. Namibia recognises the right to privacy as a fundamental human right under Article 13 of the Namibian Constitution. The two NPOs had to consider the stricter rules in Germany to make sure all regulations were met.

Traffic laws are similar in both countries, with one important difference. In Namibia, cars are driving on the left side of the road and in Germany on the right side. Driving without a valid national or international driving licence is prosecutable in both countries. The legal blood-alcohol-level for drivers is 0.05 mg alcohol to 100ml blood in both countries. Substantial fines and prison sentences are imposed for driving a vehicle while exceeding this limit. All vehicle occupants are required to always wear safety belts. Road signs are different in both countries, as are road conditions and

speed limits. In Namibia, police checks are frequently carried out both at fixed checkpoints on national roads and at short notice. Here, for example, the obligation to wear a seatbelt is checked.

3.6 Emergency Management

Namibia and Germany are both stable and peaceful countries with access to health facilities. Nevertheless, the two NPOs had to consider the unlikely event of an emergency. Hence, in case of an emergency, the Light for the Children Foundation and Suni e.V. had an emergency plan. This included a definition of an emergency (sudden natural disaster, injury, accident, impending death, becoming a victim of a crime and other life-threatening situations) and the definition of a crisis (bushfire, being arrested, getting ill, mental

Photo: Gijsbertha van Rooyen, preperation workshop in Gobabis, 2022, LftC

health problems, experience of racism or sexual assault and other situations and conflicts) as well as measures. All participants received a handout with national emergency numbers and the contact details of the two NPOs. Both coordinators were aware of whom to contact in case of an emergency. The German participants had to research local emergency numbers for fire brigade, ambulance and police, because they differ in Namibia depending on your location. All group leaders had an individual phone call plan and were taught emergency procedures. Each group had one person trained in first aid. Preparation of participants from both countries included health restrictions, hygiene, immunisation and frequent medical issues. Copies of all necessary documents were made and shared online. Both embassies were informed about the groups' visits.

There were few incidents that fell under the umbrella of emergency and crisis. Some participants did not disclose important information about illnesses, putting coordinators and group leaders in alert. Overall, however, there was no emergency. The most memorable crisis event for the group was driving very close to a bush fire and feeling the heat of the fire in the car in Namibia.

4. Encounters in Namibia and in Germany

The first encounter took place in Germany. The Namibian group visited Rhineland-Palatinate for a time of approximately three weeks. The second encounter took place in Namibia. The German group visited Namibia for three and a half weeks.

4.1 Encounter in Germany

The encounter in Germany started with sightseeing and time for the Namibian group to arrive. Afterwards, the overall group had a communication workshop in which the participants reflected on how they wanted to communicate with each other during the project. Following the first days, a one-week training with Trier University and THE BLUE MIND e.V. took place, which was proceeded by a one-week job-shadowing at German educational institutions. After that, all participants attended a Suni e.V. workshop about education during the Corona pandemic. In the course of the last days, the Namibian group was alone and visited educational institutions.

Figure 3: German-Namibian team at communication workshop in Igel, 2022, Suni e.V. (Photo: Franz Pauly)

Schedule of the Study Tour in Germany

Day	Activity	Place
Day 1	Arrival / Sightseeing	Trier
Day 2 / Saturday	Sightseeing / Recreation	Trier
Day 3 / Sunday	Communication workshop	Igel
Day 4 -8	ESD-Workshop with THE BLUE MIND e.V. and Trier University	Trier & Koblenz
Day 9-10 / Weekend	Travel & Recreation	
Day 11-15	Internship at a German educational institution	at location of German partner
Day 16-17 / Weekend	Workshop Suni e.V.	Vallendar
Day 18-21	Visiting educational institutions	Trier

Figure 4: Schedule of the Study Tour in Germany 2022, Suni e.V.

Schedule of the ESD-Training

Content	Lecturer	Time in h
Background knowledge on the Sustainable Development Goals (SDGs). Background knowledge on sustainability and the concept of Education for Sustainable Development (ESD).	Suni e.V.	4
Getting to know and applying educational units on marine conservation & water protection for children in the elementary sector.	THE BLUE MIND e.V., Universität Trier	4
Visit to the extracurricular learning sites Local Agenda 21 and the "Room of Little Researchers" at the Trier City Library. Discovering and researching practical ideas for educational work. Teaching of pedagogical methods for environmental protection and marine conservation and ideas for connecting points in the everyday life of daycare centres, after-school care centres and elementary schools	Lokale Agenda 21, City Library Trier & THE BLUE MIND e.V.	8
Independent development of educational units on the topic of marine conservation & water protection for children in the elementary sector. Project management and project creation for educational units.	Suni e.V. / THE BLUE MIND e.V.	8
Excursion to the extracurricular learning site Mosellum Koblenz. Information centre with didactic material presentation. Teaching of pedagogical methods for water protection	Mosellum Koblenz & THE BLUE MIND e.V.	8
Imparting knowledge on heavy water events and resilience in flood areas. Exploring the flood model of the Geography Didactics of the University of Trier. Teaching of pedagogical methods on the topic of heavy rain events.	Universität Trier Biologiedidaktik. Geografie Didaktik & THE BLUE MIND e.V.	4
Implementation of own projects on the topic of water for the classroom in German-Namibian contexts	THE BLUE MIND e.V., Universität Trier	4

Figure 5: Schedule of the ESD training from THE BLUE MIND e.V. and Trier University 2022, Suni e.V.

4.1.1 ESD Training with THE BLUE MIND e.V. at Trier University

The group conducted a training in the field of ESD with THE BLUE MIND e.V. in cooperation with the Trier University and its department for didactics of biology. The training was coordinated by THE BLUE MIND e.V. and implemented by several lecturers of both institutions and was based on the following three Sustainable Development Goals: SDG 4 "Quality Education", SDG 13 "Climate Protection", SDG 14 "Life below water". The training included input, excursions and visits to ESD-experts and -institutions, as well as a training in project management and the development of own projects.

The immediate feedback on the training was very positive. Several times during the training, the participants expressed that they appreciated the insights and topic. A highlight was the excursion to the Mosellum in Koblenz and the learning unit with experiments and VR-glasses by THE BLUE MIND e.V. The ocean biologist from THE BLUE MIND e.V. was named as an "inspiration" and "role model" by the educators. The different lecturers gave positive feedback as well - they found the entire group to be committed and eager to learn.

Although the training was rated as very positive, it was, nevertheless, exhausting and many participants would have benefited from having a few days off before starting the internship at a German educational institution immediately afterwards.

Figure 6: ESD-Training, 2022, Trier, Suni e.V.

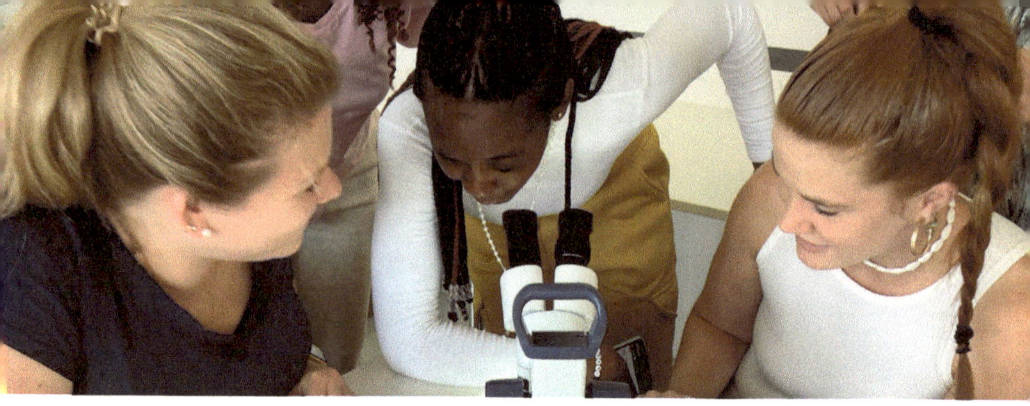

Figure 7: BioGeoLab at Trier University, 2022, Suni e.V.

4.1.2. Job shadowing at a German educational institution

The training week was followed by a week of job shadowing at an educational institution in Germany. The Namibian participants stayed at their German partners' accommodations. During this week, they received information about the educational institutions, its vision and mission, its concept and working ethic and about practical methods. They reflected with their partner on differences and on the topic of ESD. Depending on the participants wishes, they had the opportunity to speak with the coordinator via an online meeting and to exchange experiences with German colleagues in this week. Because the German group had more kindergarten educators than teachers, some Namibian teachers visited an educational institution outside their working reality. Therefore, the transfer of work-related methods was sometimes difficult, and some Namibian educators expressed the feeling of "boredom" at German kindergartens. Moreover, several Namibian guests fell ill during this week and thus, instead of five days of job shadowing, most participants only had three days at the German educational institution.

4.1.3. Challenges

Homesickness was an important factor to consider when travelling. Some of the Namibian participants had small children and others had never travelled before, two factors that made it harder for them to be away from home for three weeks. The Namibian participants formed a support group during their stay in Germany, sending each other messages and ensuring that everybody was well looked after. They all maintained regular contact with their home.

Food might be a problem when travelling to a country with a different culture as well. The German hosts were aware that their guests had other customs, and the Namibians were aware that some of their hosts ate more vegetarian dishes. Nonetheless, the Namibians were open (and even keen) to going vegetarian for a day, while the Germans were supportive and provided meat for their guests.

Hosting a guest reduced personal privacy. This responsibility for someone else and loss of privacy was a source of stress for some of the German hosts. The Namibian guests also gave the feedback that some had the feeling that they were not trusted. Here, personal conversations helped to dispel this assumption.

Even after providing a savings plan months ahead, Suni e.V. and LftC failed to ensure that each participant had enough financial support. The fact that some guests depended on the favour of the hosts, led to stress and discomfort on both parts.

Additionally, although all Namibian educators understood that German was the sole language of instruction at German educational institutions, they were sometimes surprised by their difficulty in communicating effectively in English.

Although most Namibian participants were well prepared and knew about the importance of being on schedule in German culture, some had problems being on time and had to be remembered constantly during their stay. This put additional pressure on the German organisers, group leaders and other group members.

The definition of being sick differs from culture to culture. This was also a point of dispute and discussion in the German-Namibian group. While in Germany, people often continue working until they are physically exhausted, in Namibia, greater emphasis is placed on mental and physical health. Some guests fell ill during their stay and experienced that their definition of being sick was questioned.

Personal mistakes happen. Perhaps a German host drove badly with their Namibian guest on board, or perhaps a Namibian guest showed no gratitude for the German host cooking. These mistakes put additional pressure on the partnerships. In most cases, these misunderstandings could be resolved with a

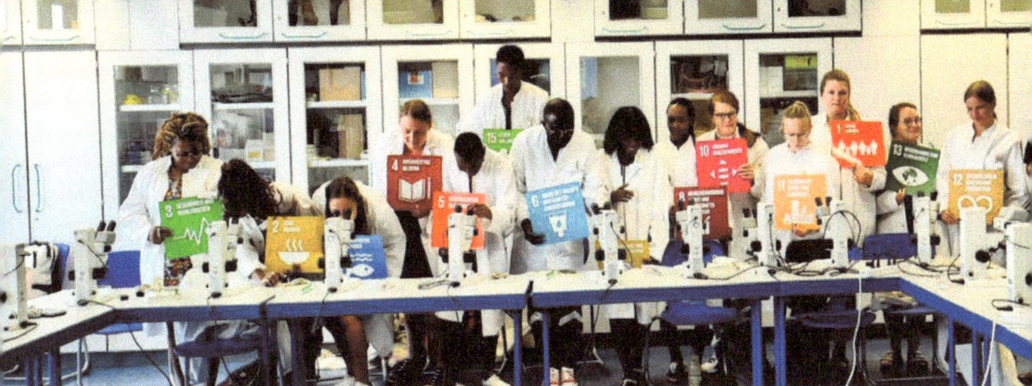

Photo: BioGeoLab at Trier University, 2022, Suni e.V.

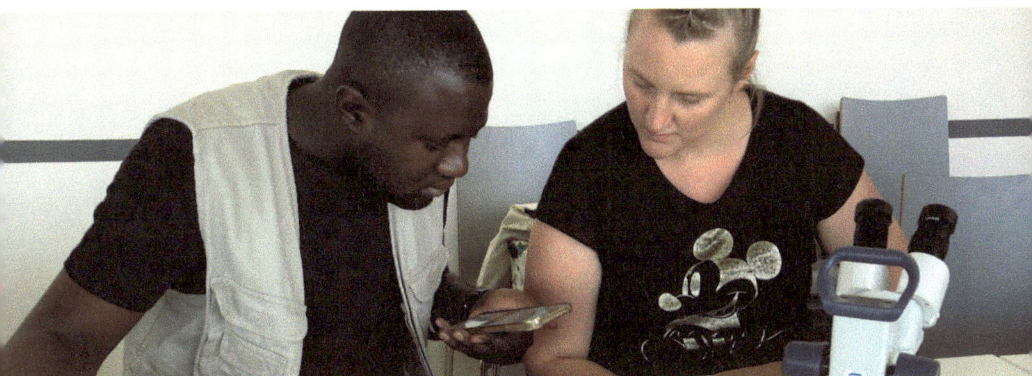

Photo: Learning about the Moselle, Koblenz, 2022, Angela Jensen

conversation and the help of others. Often, the group
leaders had to step in to address daily irritations and
challenges.

Photo: Presenting ideas at BioGeoLab, Trier University, 2022, Suni e.V.

4.2. Encounter in Namibia

The study tour in Namibia started with all participants arriving in Gobabis. After a few days of acclimatization, all participants went to the schools where their Namibian partners were employed. Here, an internship took place. After a few days, they were all picked up by transport from the Directorate of Education to attend the one-week training with the Gobabeb Namib Research Institute. After the training, the group visited Swakopmund for the weekend and departured back to Gobabis afterwards. Here, they finalized their mutual partner-projects and visited educational and political institutions in Omaheke.

Programme Study Tour Namibia

Date	Day	To Do	Accommodation
6 / 08 /	Sunday	Arrival in Gobabis	Steps Guesthouse Gobabis Evita @ Paradise Garden
7 / 08 /	Monday	Free / Grocery shopping, organizing Sim cards, tea at Gijsbertha's house	Steps Guesthouse Gobabis
8 / 08 /	Tuesday	Free / Shopping, preparing for traveling	Steps Guesthouse Gobabis
9 / 08 /	Wednesday	Travel to host	Host
10 / 08 /	Thursday	At partner school	Host
11 / 08 /	Friday	At partner school	Host
12 / 08 /	Saturday	Free	Host
13 / 08 /	Sunday	Travel to Gobabeb	Gobabeb Namib Research Institute
14 / 08 /	Monday	Training at Gobabeb	Gobabeb Namib Research Institute
15 / 08 /	Tuesday	Training at Gobabeb	Gobabeb Namib Research Institute
16 / 08 / 2023	Wednesday	Training at Gobabeb	Gobabeb Namib Research Institute
17 / 08 /	Thursday	Training at Gobabeb / Travel to Swakopmund	Jetty Self-catering Accommodation
18 / 08 /	Friday	Training in Swakopmund	Jetty Self-catering Accommodation
19 / 08 /	Saturday	Travel back to Gobabis	Steps Guesthouse Gobabis
20 / 08 /	Sunday	Free	Steps Guesthouse Gobabis
21 / 08 /	Monday	Preparation presentations 15H00 History lesson	Steps Guesthouse Gobabis
22 / 08 /	Tuesday	09H00 Min. of Education 10H00 Primary school Ben vd Walt 11H00 Light for the Children and Gobabis Project school 14H00 Cosdec 15H30 Historical Herero Cemetery	Steps Guesthouse Gobabis
23 / 08 /	Wednesday	Preparation of Presentations	Steps Guesthouse Gobabis
24 / 08 /	Thursday	09H00 Visit to the Regional Office to meet the Gouverneur of Omaheke Region 14H00 Presentation of mutual projects @ Steps Guesthouse	Steps Guesthouse Gobabis
24 / 08 /	Friday	10H00 Evaluation 13H00 Farewell lunch	Travel back home or WH

Figure 8: Schedule of the study tour in Namibia, 2023, LftC

Figure 9: The German-Namibian team at Gobabeb, 2023, LftC

4.2.1 ESD Training with the Gobabeb Namib Research Institute

After departing from Gobabis with a bus from the Ministry of Education, the group had a training at the Gobabeb Namib Research Institute. Gobabeb is located in the heart of the hyper arid Namib Desert. The mission of Gobabeb is to be a catalyst for gathering, understanding and sharing knowledge about arid environments, especially the hyper arid Namib Desert[34].

The Gobabeb team is committed to skills development of emerging environmental specialists and decision-makers. The research institute provides easy access to the three distinct ecosystems of the Namib, namely the Sand Sea to the south, the Gravel Plains to the north, and the riparian woodlands of the ephemeral Kuiseb River. These three ecosystems provide a rich diversity of arid-adapted organisms. The German-Namibian team received their training from a senior researcher with an in-depth knowledge of the Namib Desert.

4.2.2 Job shadowing at a Namibian educational institution

All German teachers were given the opportunity to shadow a Namibian school. They were linked to their Namibian exchange partner and were able to experience the Namibian school system for three days. This was definitely a big difference from what they are used to in Germany, and this provided plenty of food for discussion. The school days start early and in the afternoon, many children and teachers still have appointments related to sports or homework classes. The fact that most children can speak English made it easier for the German participants to interact during the internship.

The German participants experienced a lot of welcoming and positive feedback from colleagues at the Namibian schools. In general, these days were a very important part of the whole exchange.

Schedule ESD Training with Gobabeb

DAY 1: Monday 14th Aug 2023	Introductions and SDGs
08:30 – 09:00	Overview of Gobabeb: Introduction and overview of programme: logistics, expectations etc.
09:00 – 10:00	Critical thinking, Science and Pseudoscience
10:00 – 11:00	Refresher: What are the Sustainable Development Goals
11:15 – 13:00	Basics: Overview of Sustainable Development Goals
14:15 – 16:00	Interactive Game - Which SDGs have priority?
16:00 – 17:30	SDGs in arid countries
	Group discussion: what are the challenges in these countries
DAY 2: Tuesday 15th Aug 2023	**Society demand, Research and ESD**
08:30 – 08:40	Recap of Day 1
08:40 – 10:00	Interconnectedness of ESD, SDGs, and aspirations
10:00 – 11:00	Our Industrialized world - Systems of Production
11:15 – 12:00	Group discussion/activity - Understanding a production chain, SDGs and social justice
12:00 – 13:00	The ǂAonin people (Topnaar) of the //Khuiseb - Applying SDGs to desperately poor, marginalised groups
14:15 – 19:15	Excursion - The Lower Kuiseb agricultural system
DAY 3: Wednesday 16th Aug 2023	**Development Penalties and Nature-based solutions**
08:30 – 08:40	Recap of Day 2
08:40 – 10:00	Research for Development - What has Gobabeb done about SDGs?
10:00 – 11:00	Group discussion/activity - Citizen science as an agent for change
11:15 – 13:00	Excursion - Development Impacts on Natural systems
14:15 – 15:00	Plastics and plastic waste in our modern world
15:00 – 17:00	Confronting a global issue - How to deal with Plastic waste?
17:00 - 19:30	Excursion - The Namib Sand Sea Ecosystem and Climate Change Impacts
20:30 - 21:00	Desert Nightlife
DAY 4: Thursday 17th Aug 2023	**Climate Change and Social Justice**
07:30 – 09:30	Excursion - Tracking life in the Desert
10:20 – 10:30	Recap of Day 3
10:15 – 12:30	Group discussion/activity - Climate action and social justice
12:30 – 13:00	Closure

Figure 10: Schedule ESD-Training with Gobabeb Ramib Research Institute, 2023

Photo: LftC, Meeting with the governor of Omaheke Region, Gobabis, 2023, Suni e.V.

Photo: LftC, Welwitschia Mirablilis, Namib dessert, 2023, Suni e.V.

Figure 11: Meeting with a representative of the traditional authority of the Mbanderu, 2023, LftC

4.2.3 Challenges

Before the German participants came to Namibia, homesickness was discussed in the groups, but during their visit to Namibia, there were no complaints. The program was probably too full to give any thought to that. There were some physical complaints here and there, but nothing major or permanent. The Namibians were prepared what to do by sickness and were ready to take care of their German guests. They did their best to host them nicely and made sure they were entertained during their stay at their house.

Unfortunately, several German participants experienced corporal punishment at the Namibian schools. One of the German participants immediately contacted the Namibian coordinator of LftC and spoke to her about the fact that corporal punishment was still applied in the school. The coordinator made it clear that it was good that she has reported this. After the Germans returned, it emerged that two more participants had experienced corporal punishment. The incidents have been discussed with the relevant teachers. The Light for the Children Foundation and Suni e.V. informed the principals of the schools as well as the Directorate of Education at the Omaheke Regional council about the incidents. The incidents were then addressed by the directorate of Education. In a next exchange, this topic should be discussed beforehand more deeply.

Unfortunately, technical problems occurred quite often. This includes weak or slow Wi-Fi and no electricity for a day. Not everything works when it needs to function properly. It was a big shame that the power went off during the online presentations of the mutual projects. The only way to prevent such issues is to have a generator on hand, ready to start as soon as the power is cut.

4.3 Religion, culture, and the genocide of Namibians during the German colonial period

In past exchanges, the coordinators learned that it is important to give participants the individual time to practice their religion and room for cultural events and rituals. It has been proven to be beneficial to provide each other with insights into religions and cultures. In Germany, the whole group visited the catholic Cathedral Dom and the Liebfrauenkirche in Trier. During a visit to one of the Catholic centres in the Diocese of Trier, it made sense to exchange information about each other's cultures and religions. In Namibia, the entire group spend a day exploring the culture and religion of the OvaMbanderu and Herero with its ancestor worshipping elements. They visited a cultural-historical graveyard where many Herero people who died during the genocide are buried. Additionally, they travelled to a small fountain, a site of historical significance for the OvaMbanderu people, who established their settlement nearby due to its water source.

5. German-Namibian projects in the field of Education for Sustainable Development

During the exchange, every participant, group leader and stakeholder in Germany and Namibia was involved in a project related to SDG 4.7. "By 2030, ensure that all learners acquire the knowledge and skills needed to promote sustainable development, including, among others, through education for sustainable development and sustainable lifestyles, [...][35]". For each project, a Namibian-German team was formed. The teams had twelve months to complete the project. They had the chance to put together a project management plan. The plans were monitored by the participants themselves and the coordinators. The aim of the partner projects was to contribute to one of the SDGs, especially to SDG 4.7. and to improve the intercultural exchange by working with each other. All participants put a lot of voluntary work into their projects. Some worked independently – others needed help and support. All project groups ended up producing a hard-earned result. Communication was often difficult and cultural misunderstandings occurred. Hence, participants described working with a partner from another continent as "intense" and "challenging", but, nevertheless, also as "rewarding".

5.1 Finding German-Namibian project teams

In the exchange, the choice and composition of the groups was left to the participants themselves. At the first encounter, the participants had the chance to form German-Namibian project groups and develop a project idea during their training at the University of Trier. Based on these ideas, they formed permanent project groups to implement an ESD project.

5.2 Implementing a German-Namibian ESD project

Two teams embarked on their journey with an idea they had previously presented during the first ESD training and which had already received positive feedback. The third group went into the race with a blank paper, having the chance to do something new. Over a timeframe of one year, all three groups had to develop a project plan and give tasks and workloads to the different team members. They had to write reports, prepare presentations and to develop learning modules with classroom plans. Some had advanced experience on this, while others had none and, furthermore, some even had no computer skills. Some participants worked with shared documents and work plans, communicated via apps, and used free online services to create graphics and use photos. All groups were asked to test their learning module themselves, ask others for feedback, have it corrected by editors and other educators and were instructed to test their projects in Germany and Namibia before publishing a final learning module. Apart from one group, this instruction was implemented.

The following three projects were implemented by German-Namibian teams. Each ESD-project was first developed, then tested with learners in Germany or/ and Namibia, finalized and then published. All projects contributed to the subgoal of the SDGs 4.7. The results were presented at a hybrid event at Gobabis to peers, sponsors and members of the two organising NGOs.

5.2.1 Ocean Heroes

The German-Namibian group of the project Ocean Heroes developed a short learning unit for pre-primary education and targeted learners aged 5-7. By completing the learning unit, children are taught about the dangers of environmental pollution of the oceans. They are sensitized for clean water and motivated to protect the oceans by collecting rubbish and reducing waste. The learning module addresses SDG 6 "Clean water and sanitation", SDG 13 "Climate protection measures" and SDG 14 "Life below water".

The learning module was designed together with the German NGO THE BLUE MIND e.V.[36] and was since 2023 used in educational units for pre-primary children in Rhineland-Palatinate. The unit includes a large learning carpet representing an underwater world. The carpet has specially designed sections to collect different types of waste and was printed in two versions for German and Namibian classes.

The project was implemented with the Nossob Combined School in Witvlei, Namibia and the catholic day care centre Rebengarten in Zeltingen, Germany. The learning unit is available as download in German and English.

German version of the learning module: https://suni-ev.de/wp-content/uploads/2024/05/Lernmodul___SDG_OceanHeroes___Suni_eV_DE_Version-30-7-23.pdf

English version of the learning module: https://suni-ev.de/wp-content/uploads/2024/05/Lerning-Modul___SDG_OceanHeroes___Suni_eV_EN_30-7-23.pdf

Figure 12: Learning module in Namibia, Witvlei, 2023, Suni e.V.

Figure 13: Material in Germany 2023, Suni e.V.

Certificate for children participating in the learning module; 2023, Suni e.V.

Figure 14: Development of the Ocean Hereo learning module, Trier, 2022, Suni e.V.

5.2.2 Water filtration

"What happens to water when it is filtered through different media?" This was the central question that the members of the water filtration project sought to answer. They designed an experiment for children to illustrate how different media filter out various particles from dirty water. The group developed photo-based instructions for a water filtration experiment. The instructions are particularly easy to copy and can be used by children independently. They are embedded in a learning module with relation to the SDG 6 "Clean Water and Sanitation".

German version of the learning module: https://suni-ev.de/wp-content/uploads/2024/05/Lerning-Modul_Deutsch_SDG_Water-Filtration___Suni_eV.pdf

English version of the learning module: https://suni-ev.de/wp-content/uploads/2024/05/Lerning-Modul_English_SDG_Water-Filtration___Suni_eV.pdf:

Figure 15: Material in Germany 2023, Suni e.V.

Photo: Implementing the learning module 2023, Suni e.V.

5.2.3 Deforestation in Namibia and Germany

The German-Namibian team working on the topic of deforestation designed a learning module for secondary schools that addresses the SDG 13.3 "Build knowledge and capacity to meet climate change"[37] and the SDG 15 "Protect, restore and promote sustainable use of terrestrial ecosystems, sustainably manage forests, combat desertification, and halt and reverse land degradation and halt biodiversity loss"[38]. In this learning module, the learners should expand their knowledge on forests and their ecosystems. They should become aware of the relevance of forests for the environment and the life of various species on earth. Furthermore, they should learn about the various types of forests, their characteristics and how they are influenced by the respective climate. Additionally, they should recognize what events and actions, such as deforestation, are destroying forests around the world, thereby threatening the survival of the planet and its living inhabitants. It also teaches about country-specific characteristics of forests in Namibia and Germany.

Learners should realize that they too can contribute to protecting trees and forests. They should be encouraged to become advocates of protecting the environment and be able to implement and practice what they have learned in the project. The learning module includes a variety of methods, starting with a poster and followed by a specially designed game called "Greenscape Quest –Deforestation Detectives".

The project was implemented with the Mokganedi Tlhabanello High School in Drimiopsis, Namibia.

English version of the learning module and material: https://suni-ev.de/wp-content/uploads/2024/05/Learning-Module_Deforestation_English_2023_FINAL.pdf

Figure 16: Learning Game, 2023, Suni e.V.

5.3 Working in a German-Namibian team, conclusions and lessons learned

The German and Namibian participants approached their collaboration on a shared project differently, with notable variations primarily in communication styles and work ethics. The German participants usually communicated much more directly and often addressed issues or problems. Their communication style often seemed confrontational to the Namibian participants. In difficult situations or conflicts, the German participants often pushed forward. In contrast, the Namibian participants usually communicated more indirectly. They had a more relationship-oriented communication. In difficult situation or conflicts, the participants from Namibia were more likely to take a step back.

Not speaking English properly was an issue that could not be solved easily and became a problem in excluding participants. While the Germans placed significant emphasis on planning and outcomes with a task-oriented approach, the Namibian participants focused more on building relationships and valued the process

Figure 17: Slide from the final presentation of the learning module "Deforestation in Namibia and Germany", 2023, Suni e.V.

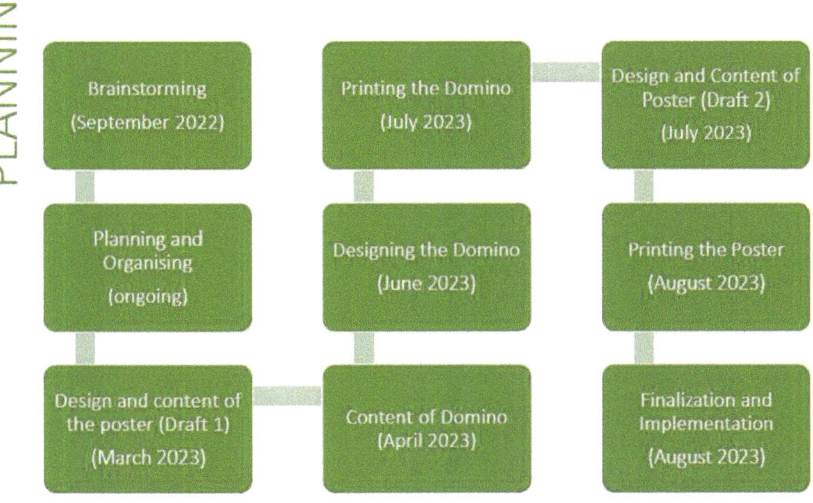

as much as the result. Additionally, whereas the German participants had a higher focus on punctuality and worked more outcome-oriented, the Namibian participants had a higher focus on inclusiveness and worked more process-oriented. These factors made it sometimes difficult to work with each other. As a result, all groups needed support by the project coordinators, and individual conversations were necessary to bring them back to the table. Of course, individual factors and characters played a role as well, and the personal chemistry between the participants in a project group was not always right. Technical difficulties occurred more in Namibia, including bad reception for online meetings or a lack of necessary apps and programs of laptops.

In the future, the two NPO will put more emphasis on the start of the projects and will make sure that all participants have the knowledge to work online successfully. They will also communicate more about different working approaches. At the beginning of the exchange program, both groups will have to do a personality test in order to have a better understanding of different learning and behaviour styles.

Given that nearly all of the project work was conducted online by young people who hardly knew each other, had limited experience in SDG project work, came from diverse cultural backgrounds and undertook the work on a voluntary basis, their achievements are all the more remarkable. The implementation of the mutual projects is highly valuable, as it results in the creation of lesson plans that are available to other educators and hence, enriching the education sector.

Photo: *Childrens books about ESD, 2023, Suni e.V.*

6. Monitoring, reflection, and evaluation

Several methods were used to monitor and evaluate the exchange: a questionnaire, a daily group diary, reflection reports, personal conversations, an online survey and group discussions. The feedback prompted the coordinators to change certain events or to add other features.

6.1 Monitoring

Both coordinators from Light for the Children Foundation and Suni e.V. held regular online meetings. In this way, they could keep each other up to date and monitor, via shared access, each other's bookings and itineraries for workshops and study tours. Reflections and group discussions on the workshops were used to improve the ongoing process and, wherever possible, the participants ideas were incorporated

To ensure that participants worked on their projects, several personal conversations were held, and the coordinators sent regular reminders. To ensure participants stayed in contact with each other, they were given checklists to log their communication. Some were sent regular WhatsApp reminders by their coordinators to contact their partners. A group diary during the study tours showed the activities and reflections from each day, and personal reports and conversations provided an inside look into the program. The participants made important suggestions for improving the program, such as shifting the daily reflections to the mornings and including more leisure time.

6.2 Follow-up workshops and evaluation

Both groups participated in two follow-up workshops: one following the Namibian group's visit to Germany and the other after the German group's visit to Namibia. These workshops were utilized for reflection and group discussions. To see how much knowledge the participants acquired about the other country and its educational system, all of them had to complete a simple questionnaire with questions about the two countries. Additionally, an evaluation off the overall program was done with i-EVAL, an online based survey system for international exchanges. Unfortunately, many participants had problems using this online based tool and only six completed the survey.

In order to evaluate the program and identify its effects, all information from the workshop, diaries and written reflection reports were compiled.

7. Outcome and Impact

In designing the exchange, several anticipated outcomes were named to be achieved with this program. This included the improvement of intercultural competences and the gaining of knowledge. Overall, the exchange should qualify participants to educate ESD. Moreover, the produced projects should reach children in Germany and in Namibia and support a change in our societies.

Not all results can be made visible with the evaluation and reflection methods mentioned in chapter seven. In particular, the long-term effects are not apparent and can only be anticipated. This chapter therefore focuses on the measures carried out in correlation with the planned outcomes. Therefore, we are focusing on

a)   an increase in knowledge about Germany and Namibia,

b)   an increase in intercultural competencies and reduction of stereotypes,

c)   possible insights into foreign education systems and exchange of educational methods,

d)   the qualifications of educators as multipliers for ESD and

e)   personal impacts.

On top of this, the group leaders and organisers present an insight into their personal learning experiences during the exchange. Finally, all results of the exchange that were not planned are presented in the last part of this chapter.

7.1   Gaining knowledge about Germany and Namibia

Knowledge about another country includes knowing the political system, which languages are spoken, how the economy is structured, fauna and flora as well as daily customs in the country. In general, the evaluations show that, the participants had the opportunity to get an insight into each other's country and that they used this insight to learn and observe. All 14 participants proved they could answer significantly more questions about Germany/Namibia and their respective school systems after the two-year period than before. Even if their visit was a year ago, the participants remembered political structures and numbers or general information about both countries. These results were supported in the discussion groups in Germany and in Namibia, where participants expressed that they gained much knowledge. They identified the job shadowing, the recreation days and the preparation workshops as most important in the context of gaining knowledge about the other country. The trainings were a base of knowledge too, but more on an expert level. For example, the whole group learned about venomous animals and the ecosystem in the Namib Desert, which was new to all.

7.2   Increase in intercultural competences and reduction of stereotypes

Intercultural competences are a combined setting of knowledge (described in chapter 8.1), skills, attitudes and experience[39].

Most participants have not travelled much. Many did not even have a valid passport. Beside the group leaders, none had been in the other country before.

During the exchange, most participants of both country groups acquired or improved their language skills to communicate with the team members of the other country. Some improved their English even to an impressive extent. Most participants stated that they had improved communication and problem-solving skills and that they had learned to adapt. One example was the adaptation to different cuisines and the adaptation to use different infrastructures in both countries. All of them gained cultural knowledge, although the experiences are very diverse with some expressing that they feel like a new world opened to them and others saying they only learned minimal additional information about the culture in the other country. The biggest change in perception was when it came to stereotypes. Here, many participants were confronted with their biases and expressed that they had to reflect on their assumptions. For instance, some German participants were surprised that the Namibians were so attached to their smart-phones and impressed how professional their social media presence was. In contrast, some Namibians were disappointed that German schools were not up-to-date when it came to ESD. One participant expressed:

A change in attitude could also been seen after the group had a heated discussion about "being sick". After initially declaring that one should go to work unless one "falls over", the German group stepped back and actually exclaimed that the approach from

> „They [the teachers from the German school] did not know about Education for Sustainable Development. Germany is supposed to be advanced and developed. But they did not know."

Quote from a teacher after the study trip to Germany, EE, 2022

their Namibian team members to stay at home, even if one "just" feels ex-hausted, was more health-oriented. Numerous such discussions could be observed from the group leaders and organisers. Overall, the participants also managed difficult situations, such as having limited water supply or travelling in unknown territory, and they all gained more experience working in international diverse groups. Thus, one can say with confidence that the participants improved their intercultural competences and reduced their stereotypes. However, there is also room for improvement: In this context, the Namibian participants ex-pressed that they had wished to have more contact with cultural events in Germany.

The German participants expressed the same wish. When it came to the preparation phase, they would have benefited to get more information about the different language groups in Namibia before their journey to Namibia, and they had wished to have more time for exploring the foreign country.

7.3 Insight into education systems and exchange of educational methods

The job shadowing was described as a lesson learned by many, but not all. Due to the group being very diverse, the visited institution did not fit with the profession of the educator and hence, some educators could not gain many insights into their field of profession as they had wished to. The exchange of methods was therefore also more difficult. Nonetheless, the job shadowing brought an important insight into working ethics and into society.

The job shadowing provided insights into how educational institutions in both countries could implement ESD. Considering the environments at the schools they visited, many German participants recognised that ESD is not a priority in Namibia, where students must first meet their basic needs. In comparison, Namibian participants learned that in Germany, ESD is not included in many educational institutions even though they have the resources.

The job shadowing should be more closely aligned with the participants' preferences in the future. To this end, participant pairings should be based on their professions.

7.4 Qualification of educators as multipliers for ESD

The two trainings in the field of Education for Sustainable Development were regarded as highlights by all participants. Whereas the training in Germany with THE BLUE MIND e.V. and the University of Trier had a bigger impact on the Namibians, the training with the Gobabeb Research Institute was identified as the highlight by German participants. The trainings were described as "excellent", "inspiring" and "unique". Both trainings were assessed to have a balanced mix of theoretical input and practical training. Many participants became aware about consumption and ecological impacts of one's actions during the trainings. The trainings led to a behavioural change for many participants. For example, some participants stopped using single-use items such as cups, while others became politically active by attending events on Education for Sustainable Development. They implemented projects or lessons on different topics they had learned during the trainings before. Some stayed in contact with the organisations that implemented the trainings.

Although the evaluations clearly show that all participants have enhanced their knowledge and methods in the field of ESD and applied these methods in the short term, it was not possible within the scope of the evaluation to determine whether these methods are used sustainably in their daily work or if the educators are effectively acting as multipliers. To address this knowledge gap, the organisers once again sought the expertise of the Trier University. In this context, a master's student will carry out a data collection to find out whether this goal has been achieved in the long term. The results are expected in 2025.

7.5 Personal impact

As discussed in the follow-up workshops, the personal impact was the area that yielded the most positive results. The exchange led to a change in behaviour for many participants. Most expressed that they were more cautious with ecological decisions or became political active by joining (first) demonstrations. The exchange had both direct and indirect impacts on personal future decisions, such as writing one's Master's thesis on aspects of the German and Namibian educational systems or planning to visit the other country again. However, the most frequently named impact in both national groups was "friendships". Over the course of two years, friendships were formed and strengthened both within the national groups and the international group. Emotional connection is a foundation for empathy and therefore might lead to solidarity and equality. Participants are expressing a desire to make these connections lasting. That is why the organisers believe that this result has the greatest potential to bring about change.

Figure 19: German participants answered the question what personal long-term results they see after participating in the exchange, 2023, Suni e.V.

7.6 Unplanned outcome

In addition to the planned outcomes, there were also some unplanned outcomes of the German-Namibian exchange of Educators. The organising parties observed an increase in the political engagement of participants, evidenced by their participation in additional events. Many participants used the opportunity to network and form new cooperations. Additionally, the project strengthened the collaboration among all partner NPOs included in the project. This subchapter gives a detailed overview of the unplanned results.

7.6.1 Getting involved: Accra, Mainz and Kigali

During the exchange, the organisers shared calls for training courses and public events on ESD and the SDGs. Many participants took the chance to become active and attend events.

The African German Youth Office (AGYO) hosted its first ever workshop since its establishment in 2020. One Namibian participant represented Suni e.V. during this event. The workshop took place from 31st October until 3rd November 2022 in Accra, Ghana. The focus of the workshop was on youth exchange programs and youth networking between Germany and various African countries. Therefore, 30 participants from Germany and different African countries took part in the workshop. They represented different non-profit organisations from their respective countries during the event. The workshop focussed on strengthening multipliers for the SDG's and creating awareness about the Agenda 2030.

Two German participants joined the Parliamentary evening in the Mainz state parliament with the title "Sustainability needs a new cooperation". They represented the group and discussed with stakeholders and other NPOs.

One Namibian participant from the Team of the Ocean Heroes applied with three Suni e.V. members to participate at an SDG training of the AGYO to expand the project to a learning module for older children. The group was accepted and received a one-week training from experts about project management and the SDGs in Kigali, Ruanda[40]. The group developed a project called "Aquatic Guardians" to address the SDG 14 "life below water".

7.6.2 Teaching others

During the encounter in Germany, a learning module about the SDGs was designed with students from Trier University. It is an open-source document and can be downloaded[41].

Several Namibian participants took part in a program of Suni e.V. to teach German students about Namibia. They engaged in online discussions with German learners and shared their insights as experts on the impact of German-Namibian history on their personal lives. In this way, approximately 200 German students benefited from the insights of the Namibian teachers.

Several participants presented the exchange and the developed projects at events. At Trier University (Germany), the exchange was promoted by a German and a Namibian participant at their ESD-day for teacher training students. Suni e.V. was also invited to present the exchange at the ESD day for teachers in Rheinböllen (Germany) and produced a presentation with all participants for the SDG Workshop of the German-Namibian Society.

7.6.3 Academic research projects

A mental health project for teachers from the University of Kaiserslautern-Landau (Germany) accompanied the participants of the exchange. In the project, the participants kept short diaries on their smartphones about stress, self-care and daily events. The results were intended to provide information about well-being and short-term stress phases during an exchange and (possible) resources for coping with them. Unfortunately, due to a very low response rate, it was not possible to analyse the data as the anonymity of the participants could no longer be guaranteed. For possible future app-based projects on mental health in the context of exchange formats, greater attention should be paid in advance to the technical requirements and the time to participate.

The two German participants, who were still university students, decided to write their Master thesis about a German-Namibian topic. One topic addressed the question of what children in Namibia and Germany know about climate change. Children in Trier, Germany and Witvlei, Namibia were asked about their ideas on climate change. To do her research, she was supported by Namibian teachers she had met during her short job shadowing. The other thesis examined the perceptions of German and Namibian primary school pupils on the topic of water and water purification through drawings and interviews with the children.

7.6.4 Forming a school partnership

During the encounter in Germany, one of the schools hosting a teacher from Namibia, the Freie Montessorischule Landau, decided to start a school partnership with the teacher's school, Tlhabanello High School. They applied for funding with the German Development policy school exchange program ENSA (Entwicklungspolitisches Schulaustauschprogramm). Two initiation trips took already place in June and October 2024 with teachers and students from both schools visiting each other. It is intended to continue this partnership[42]. The joint school partnership has a Facebook and a GoFundMe page.

7.6.5 Establishment of support groups for organisations

As there were a lot of bureaucratic peculiarities in relation to funding from the AGYO during the implementation of the exchange format, the German NPO Suni e.V. networked with stakeholders who also carried out an exchange with the AGYO. A position paper was drawn up in a group of 14 organisations. This included proposals for the AGYO's Teams Up! program aimed at minimising administrative hurdles, enhancing the involvement of southern partners, and overall improving user-friendliness. Suni e.V. and three other stakeholders presented the position paper to the management of the AGYO.

A second small support group was formed with actors from three German-Namibian partnerships. Here, the participants exchanged concrete information on the implementation of their trips and supported each other.

7.6.6 Becoming an activist

Through the exchange, one Namibian participant met the Rhineland-Palatinate Development Policy Network e.V. and she participated together with the president of Light for the Children Foundation in a German-wide campaign called "Voices of the climate crisis"[43]. Her input about climate change was used to make people from the Global South and their perspectives on climate change more visible in German society.

7.6.7 Connecting with political decision makers

The day before the Germans departed from Gobabis, the group leader of the Namibian team met with the Governor of the Omaheke Region to discuss the status of the Namibian-German exchange. He invited the entire group to his office the following morning for a welcome reception. He wanted to know from each participant where they worked and what degree they had. He also shared his vision for the Omaheke region, focusing on the cultivation of local crops and vegetables to reduce malnutrition among young children. He also spoke highly of Suni e.V. and the Light for the Children school and Foundation and their work. This was a great opportunity for the group to connect with a political decision maker.

7.6.8 Awards

The German-Namibian team developing the "Ocean Heroes" project will be recognized by the Catholic Church in the diocese of Trier, as the learning module they created has been implemented in several Catholic kindergartens. The group will receive a recognition for their voluntary work at the end of 2024. Suni e.V. will receive an award from the German UNESCO commission in October 2024. Four participants will receive a proof of competence from the German federal state of Rhineland-Palatinate.

Figure 20: Poster from the "Voices of the climate crises" - campagne, Trier, 2023, Lokale Agenda 21

8. Lessons Learned

This chapter is a personal conclusion. It shows the individual learning experiences of the organisers and group leaders. The lessons learned, as outlined in this chapter, pertain to two distinct levels. Firstly, it highlights the areas that have been successful and should be preserved. Conversely, it identifies those areas deemed critical and in need of enhancement by the individual authors.

8.1 Lessons learned from the organisers' perspective

From an organisational perspective, preparation is key. Considering country specific holidays and seasons and speaking with people, who have already implemented a similar project, was for sure one of the best preparations. By trying to be prepared and foreseeing problems, the organisers gave their best to facilitate the exchange program.

Due to the shared use of documents and finances, most misunderstandings from a previous exchange were reduced. Therefore, a solid base of trust between the organisers existed and proved to be valuable. Nonetheless, organisers should reflect their stereotypes and biases in the same way as the participants and make sure that they overcome presumptions and are sensitive to racism, power imbalances between the NPOs or diversity issues.

Lesson learned from a Namibian perspective:

"Don't take communication for granted. Don't assume we are all adults and capable of managing simply because we can communicate. In such a diverse group, it is essential to be very explicit about the tasks, the rules, and the expectations. Communication is a skill, and we can all improve at it. The importance of communication is something I experienced once again. In a future exchange, I want to emphasise the topic of communication more. Miscommunication causes many unnecessary conflicts and problems.

Another lesson I learned is the importance of having a plan B or C in case the first plan does not work out.

My personal highlight was spread throughout the program and it was always related to the differences in culture. For example, there was a moment when one of the German guests realised that the taxi driver was not keeping his word and arrived 1.5 hours later because he needed to pick up some more people. Here in Namibia, we are more dependent on other people.

Or the deep desire for meat during a meal for our Namibian group, who feel not completely satisfied with a vegetarian meal. These moments reminded me of how accustomed we are to certain things and how beneficial it is to still work together as a diverse group. Meeting halfway and compromising so that the work can be done is key. I greatly enjoyed the moments when I saw recognition and understanding in the eyes of the German group, and we were able to talk about the cultural differences. Even though the diversity was enormous, the reward of completing the exchange together in peace is a victory!
Diversity doesn't mean there is no unity!"

Lesson learned from a German perspective:

" We gained a great deal of valuable experience during the organisation of this exchange. Maintaining contact with everyone and ensuring that mutual projects are well-supervised proved to be crucial. Going forward, group leaders will focus on overseeing the group and administrative tasks, allowing ESD projects to have dedicated supervision. In future exchanges, we will proactively address child protection and corporal punishment early in the preparation phase, ensuring that everyone is well-informed about the legal frameworks in both countries.

My most significant takeaway is the importance of effective communication: I recognised opportunities to enhance communication both on my part and within the international group. In hindsight, taking a break when sensing any irritations would have been beneficial. Although the tight schedule was a challenge, it reinforced the need for flexibility. In future exchanges, I aim to create more opportunities for the group to discuss any concerns, even if it means adjusting the program. I will also enhance transparency regarding myself and clearly communicate the regulations established by the project donors.

The educators from Germany and Namibia work best when they are passionate about a subject and have the freedom to implement their own ideas and visions related to it. Our task as organisers is to support them and help clear any obstacles in their path. This approach has been successful, and I intend to continue it in the future."

8.2 Lessons learned from the group leaders' perspective

The group leaders had a dual role in the exchange. On the one hand, they took part in all activities and jointly developed ESD projects and materials, and on the other hand, they had management tasks in the areas of group dynamics, monitoring and financial accounting. They were the contact persons for personal problems and individual conflicts. Here are their perspectives:

"My role as a group leader included being a contact person for the two coordinators during the trips of the exchange program. Before the exchange the communication with the organisers was over mail and WhatsApp and some online zoom-meetings before the exchange. During the trip in Germany there was a face-to-face-meeting with the German coordinator every day or at least every second day, in Namibia the program involved more travelling, therefore the contact to the Namibian coordinator was less frequent than in Germany. In Germany my role as a group leader also included to know the timetable, where to go and when and sometimes plan how to get there by public transport and making sure everybody leaves on time. In parts, it also included to keep an eye on the budget and therefore arranging with the group where and what to eat or collecting receipts. As everyone has different preferences, this can be quite time-consuming.

I was also a contact person for the German group for their concerns, needs and wishes. Before the Namibian group visited Germany, there weren't too many questions. When the trip to Namibia came closer, a lot more questions arise, topics were for example on packing or how to protect themselves from mosquitos. During the trip to Namibia, I tried to keep an open ear for (personal) conflicts between the group members, but also trying to not engage too much in those conflicts and take a step back. Some participants found it hard to adapt to the new culture and environment, especially at the homestays, so we talked over the phone what can be done to make them feel better. The communication with the German group was also over WhatsApp, sometimes phone-calls and in order to prepare for the trip to Namibia some few online-meetings after official meetings.

As for communication with the whole group, it was sometimes difficult, because not everybody was there or the rooms of the accommodation were not always close to each other, so a lot of communication during the exchange phase was also over a WhatsApp to make sure everyone is on the same page, which worked well in Germany, but not always in Namibia. Apart from reading more about the partner country I did not specifically prepare for the role as a group leader in this project, because I stepped in for another person, which might have been a bit naive. I was working as a youth leader when I was in school and had some leading functions in university groups and associations as well. My experience with Namibia were two internships for about a year in total. A big difference was that my former experience in leading groups was rather teamwork, including the decision-making, and there were meetings only once or twice a week and you were (mostly) not staying together as it was the case for this exchange program. Also the intercultural setting was new for me, in my internships I was working in smaller teams or on my own. I think my professional knowledge in psychological topics, especially on coping with stress, helped me in assisting the German group well, but not so much in the intercultural setting.

Being a group leader and member at the same time made it hard to be taken seriously and listened to sometimes and therefore some tasks (filling out evaluations with the whole group, getting receipts) were not fulfilled adequately. The awareness about stress and my own capacities was sometimes also an obstacle, because I had to (knowingly) exceed my limits sometimes. So I would say that a lot of resilience is needed for a group leader, especially in terms of interpersonal relationships, not taking things too personally or seriously. I had some experience with travelling in groups but realized that not every group is as considerate about everyone and made sure everyone was alright as I was used to. During the exchange, I realized that it can be quite challenging to be around with a lot of persons with a lot of different expectations. I guess with this combination of personality types, everyone had to step back from his/her usual being to make sure everything works out. Unfortunately, I am not sure if this made the quieter group members falling under the wheels sometimes.

Keeping the mentioned matters in mind for future projects, I would suggest considering the following:

- Prepare for your role in terms of culture and power relations. What does it mean to be a group leader in your own culture, but also what does it mean in the other culture (also consider age and gender)?

- Be prepared to make yourself unpopular with some announcements and instructions to the group. There will be some participants who may accept you as group leader and at the same time be your friends, and some who have a hard time mixing these roles, so try to not take it personally.

- Ask people in advance if they need more guidance, or if they might feel that much advice feels for them too much like being mothered.

- Try to not put all tasks on you. As it is sometimes difficult to get everyone together in the heat of the moment, it is good to delegate some tasks according to preferences in advance. If someone likes cooking, that person might be enjoying planning the meals together with someone who is good in finances.

- Try to look out for quieter persons and make sure they are also alright."

"My role as a group leader was to guide and assist participants if there were minor disputes or confusions, to submit receipts for purchases made by participants, to listen to participants if they needed someone to talk to, and to take the lead if presenters needed someone from the group to clarify some information for them.

"It boosted my confidence and made me realise skills that I never knew I had."

A group leader, 2023

We had several separate meetings with the organisers, sometimes in person and sometimes online, where we shared our opinions about issues affecting participants. The organisers supported us and encouraged us to be open when we needed guidance from them, and I felt our opinions were highly valued. The communication channels with the organisers were open, and we could contact them without hesitation.

During our separate meetings with organisers, there was a lot of open communication about how to handle issues if they arose. There were a few times when we were advised on how to handle finances, which was very helpful.

I had a very pleasant experience with the whole exchange program. It boosted my confidence and made me realise skills that I never knew I had, like conflict management, listening skills, and being part of a group while having fun at the same time.

A group leader must be someone that people can rely on, someone who can listen, understands how culture shock and homesickness can manifest, lends a helping hand, and must ask for help if they do not have solutions to problems."

9. Conclusion

This descriptive report outlines the planning and implementation process of the German-Namibian Educator Exchange conducted by Light for the Children Foundation from Namibia and Suni e.V. from Germany in 2022 and 2023. In addition to detailing the objectives of the exchange, the preparation, and participant selection, the authors describe each phase and its implementation. They provide insights into training programs in Germany and Namibia and group projects in Education for Sustainable Development. The report discusses the methods used to reflect on and evaluate the exchange before presenting the results, offering a resource for others as both inspiration and guidance for avoiding similar challenges. Ultimately, it prompts the following question: Was it worth it?

When we consider the environmental impact, we refer to the *ecological footprint*. Meanwhile, the term *social handprint* is used to describe actions promoting a good and sustainable life for all in line with the Sustainable Development Goals. At the conclusion of this two-year project, Suni e.V. and Light for the Children Foundation must reflect on the relationship between the ecological footprint and the social handprint.

On paper, most targets for the German-Namibian exchange have been met, with participants gaining knowledge about each other's countries, enhancing their intercultural competencies, and reflecting on their stereotypes. Many participants experienced a shift in perspective and noteworthy learning progress. They developed new learning modules and demonstrated their qualifications to implement ESD projects with children in Namibia and Germany. The exchange has benefited not only 14 educators, but also reached hundreds of children in both countries. Additionally, several unplanned outcomes emerged: participants became politically active, formed new partnerships, presented their projects internationally, and initiated various social and ecological events, none of which would have occurred without this exchange.

Participants have been recognized and awarded for their voluntary work.

Yet, there are downsides: air travel and other transport have led to environmental harm that would not have occurred without the exchange. Future flights for newly formed school partnerships and return visits may add to this ecological impact. Moreover, while educators indicate a willingness to change behaviour and teach ESD, the lasting effect is uncertain. We cannot be sure that postcolonial perspectives have been entirely dismantled, nor that stereotypes will not re-emerge. Communication challenges and difficulties remain unresolved and could hinder future interactions. Therefore, drawing a definitive conclusion is challenging.

Suni e.V. and Light for the Children Foundation believe that the social handprint currently outweighs the ecological footprint. The exchange benefits participants and their communities with potential to shift perspectives and contribute to saving our planet. However, this assessment might evolve, prompting a close examination. The exchange format should be improved and redesigned to minimise its ecological impact and fully achieve all objectives. The job-shadowing must better align with participants' professions, and bilateral project work should be closely supervised to ensure productive issue resolution in German-Namibian project teams. Alternative options, such as exchanges without flights, should be discussed. Although both NPOs have ideas for a digital exchange, they are unsure if this would compromise the essential outcomes.

Ultimately, the most enduring achievement of the exchange is the friendships that have developed between educators from Germany and Namibia. These emotional bonds have the potential to significantly contribute to a prosperous and sustainable future for all involved.

Figure 21: German and Namibian educators at Gobabeb, 2022, LftC

Literature

1 United Nations (2016). Transforming our world, The Agenda 2030 für sustainable Development. p. 19, Available at: https://sustainabledevelopment.un.org/content/documents/21252030%20Agenda%20for%20Sustainable%20Development%20web.pdf (Access 6.5.2024)

2 United Nations (2016) Transforming our world, The Agenda 2030 für sustai.nable Development. p. 28, Available at: https://sustainabledevelopment.un.org/content/documents/21252030%20Agenda%20for%20Sustainable%20Development%20web.pdf (Access 6.5.2024)

3 United Nations (2016). Transforming our world, The Agenda 2030 für sustainable Development. p. 19, Available at: https://sustainabledevelopment.un.org/content/documents/21252030%20Agenda%20for%20Sustainable%20Development%20web.pdf (Access 6.5.2024)

4 UN (2015). Transforming Our World: The 2030 Agenda for Sustainable Development. Resolution Adopted by the General Assembly on 25 September 2015, 42809, 1-13.

5 Federal Ministry of Education and Research (2017). National Action Plan on Education for Sustainable Development. Available at: https://www.bne-portal.de/bne/shareddocs/downloads/files/bmbf_nap_bne_en_screen_2.html (Access 1.11.2023)

6 Ministerium für Bildung (Hrsg.) (2020). Schulgesetz (SchulG). Mainz. Available at: https://grundschule.bildung-rp.de/rechts-grundlagen/schulgesetz.html (Access 1.11.2023)

7 Ministerium für Wirtschaft, Verkehr, Landwirtschaft und Weinbau Rheinland-Pfalz (2021). Nachhaltigkeitsstrategie Rheinland-Pfalz, Indikatorenbericht 2021. Mainz.

8 Christian Wittlich (2021). Außerschulische Bildung für nachhaltige Entwicklung. Eine qualitative und quantitative Studie zur Lernortlandschaft in Rheinland-Pfalz unter besonderer Berücksichtigung der Wirksamkeit von BNE-Bildungsmaßnahmen. Universität Koblenz-Landau, S. 89

9 Netzwerk Bildung für nachhaltige Entwicklung Rheinland-Pfalz (2024). Bildung für nachhaltige Entwicklung (BNE) in Rheinland-Pfalz. Available at: https://nachhaltigkeit.bildung-rp.de/bne-schulen.html (Access 1.11.2023)

10 Lokale Agenda 21 (2021). Fortbildung zur Fachkraft BNE im Elementarbereich. Trier, Available at: https://la21-trier.de/bildungsangebote/bne-fachkraft/?cn-reloaded=1 (Access 1.11.2023)

11 Pädagogisches Landesinstitut Rheinland-Pfalz (2021). Bildung für nachhaltige Entwicklung (BNE), Aktuelles. Mainz, Available at: https://nachhaltigkeit.bildung-rp.de/ (Access 1.11.2023)

12 Ministry of Environment, Forestry & Tourism (2019). National Environmental Education and Education for Sustainable Development Policy. Windhoek

13 Damaris Braune and Alisa Volkmann (7.12.2022). Namibian Teachers become pioneers of Education for Sustainable Development. Conservation Namibia, Available at: https://conservationnamibia.com/blog/namibian-teachers-pioneer-esd-2022.php (Access 31.12.2021)

14 Ministry of Environment, Forestry & Tourism (2019). National Environmental Education and Educa-tion for Sustainable Development Policy. Windhoek, p. iv

15 UNESCO (2020). Namibian Change Projects, Available at: https://sustainabilityteachers.org/change-projects/namibia/ (Access 31.12.2021)

16 NaDEET (2021). Teach for ESD. NaDEET, Available at: https://nadeet.org/teach-esd (Access 31.12.2021)

17 Gobabeb Namib Research Institute (2021). Gobabeb Namib Research Institute. Available at: https://gobabeb.org/ (Access 31.5.2021)

18 Gobabeb Namib Research Institute (2021). Gobabeb Namib Research Institute. Available at: https://gobabeb.org/ (Accessed: 31.5.2021)

19 Paavo Järvensivu et al. (2018). Global Sustainable Development Report 2019 drafted by the Group of independent scientists. Invited background document on economic transformation, to chapter: Trans-formation: The Economy. Available at: https://sustainabledevelopment.un.org/globalsdreport/2019 (Accessed: 31.12.2021)

20 "Footprints are the environmental and social impacts of the processes that sustain us. (These processes sustain us by directly or indirectly supplying every good and service we buy or experience.) Handprints are changes to environmental and social impacts that we cause outside of our footprints."
Greg Norris (2018). Footprints and Handprints: The Ripple Effects of our Presence. Available at: https://trimtab.living-future.org/trim-tab/issue-35/footprints-and-handprints-the-ripple-effects-of-our-presence/ (Access 31.12.2021)

21 Climate Chance Connection (2019). ECOLOGICAL HANDPRINT. Available at: https://climatechangeconnection.org/wp-content/uploads/2019/03/Ecological-Handprint-Backgrounder.pdf (Access 1.9.2024)

22 Engagement Global (2016). Funding Guideline weltwärts - Extracurricular exchange projects in the context of Agenda 2030. Available at: https://www.weltwaerts.de/files/media/dokumente_dc/en/Begegnungen/Publications/wwB_Funding_guideline_exchange_projects.pdf (Access 4.5.2024)

23 United Nations (2016). Transforming our world,
The Agenda 2030 für sustainable Development. p. 19,
Available at: https://sustainabledevelopment.un.org/
content/documents/21252030%20Agenda%20for%20
Sustainable%20Development%20web.pdf (Access 6.5.2024)

24 UN (2015). Transforming Our World: The 2030 Agenda
for Sustainable Development. Resolution Adopted by the
General Assembly on 25 September 2015, 42809, 1-13.

25 Magdalena Zatylna, Dominik Mosiczuk (2019). Checklist
„Diversity in Youth Exchange Checklist". DPJW

26 In accordance with the terminology of the Namibian
Ministry of Education, Arts and Culture the term *home
language* is used here instead of mother tongue. The term
refers to the language that is predominantly spoken in the
person's household.

27 UNICEF (2023). HIV/Aids in Namibia. Available at:
https://www.unicef.de/informieren/projekte/afrika-2244/
namibia-19312/aids-aufklaerung/12876 (Access 31.12.2023)

28 The Norwegian Students' and Academics' International
Assistance Fund (2022). How To Communi-cate The World A
SOCIAL MEDIA GUIDE FOR VOLUNTEERS AND TRAVELERS from
RadiAid & Barbie Saviour. Available at: www.radiaid.com/
social-media-guide/ (Access 8.9.2023)

29 Project Everyone and the Global Goals Campaign (2022).
WELCOME TO THE WORLD'S LARG-EST LESSON!. Available
at: https://worldslargestlesson.globalgoals.org/ (Access
1.3.2022)

30 Bundesministerium für Familien, Senioren, Frauen und
Jugend (2022). Bundeskinderschutzgesetz. Berlin

31 Republic of Namibia (2019). Child Care Protection Act 3 of
2015. Windhoek. Available at: https://www.lac.org.na/laws/
annoSTAT/Child%20Care%20and%20Protection%20Act%20
3%20of%202015.pdf (Access 10.12.2023)

32 Republic of Namibia (2019). Child Care Protection Act 3
of 2015. Windhoek. Available at: https://www.lac.org.na/laws/
annoSTAT/Child%20Care%20and%20Protection%20Act%20
3%20of%202015.pdf (Access 10.12.2023)

33 Republic of Namibia (1990). Namibian Constitution.
p. 12, Available at: https://www.lac.org.na/laws/annoSTAT/
Namibian%20Constitution.pdf (Access 10.12.2023)

34 Gobabeb Namib Research Institute (2022). Welcome
to Gobabeb. Available at: https://gobabeb.org/ (Access
12.8.2022)

35 UN (2023). SDG Indicators, Goal 4. Ensure inclusive
and equitable quality education and promote lifelong
learning opportunities for all. Available at: https://unstats.
un.org/sdgs/metadata/?Text=&Goal=4&Target=4.7 (Acess
10.9.2023)

36 Bagusche, Frauke Dr. (2024). THE BLUE MIND e.V.
Available at: https://thebluemind.org/ (Access 12.12.2023)

37 United Nations (2017). Make the SDGs a Reality.
Availabale at: sustainabledevelopment.un.org (Access
10.9.2023

38 United Nations (2017). Make the SDGs a Reality. Avaibale
at: sustainabledevelopment.un.org (Access 10.9.2023)

39 Monash University (2024). What is intercultural
competence, and why is it important? Available at: https://
www.monash.edu/arts/monash-intercultural-lab/about-the-
monash-intercultural-lab/what-is-intercultural-competence
(Access 12.12.2023)

40 DAJW (19.06.2023). Training zur praktischen Umsetzung
der SDGs. Available at: https://www.deutsch-afrikanisches-
jugendwerk.de/de/mediathek/nachricht/training-zur-
praktischen-umsetzung-der-sdgs.html (Access 17.8.2024)

41 Barbara Scharfbillig (2022). How to make the world a
better place. Available at: https://suni-ev.de/wp-content/
uploads/2023/01/Lernmodul_Wie-ich-die-Welt-verbessern-
kann_SDGs_101_DEUTSCH_Suni_eV.pdf (Access 29.5.2024)

42 Stadt Landau (21.6.2024). Partnerschaft mit Schule
in Namibia: Schülerinnen und Schüler der Mokganedi
Tlhabanello High School und der Freien Montessorischule
Landau zu Gast im Rathaus. Available at: https://www.
landau.de/Verwaltung-Politik/Pressemitteilungen/
Partnerschaft-mit-Schule-in-Namibia-Sch%C3%BClerinnen-
und-Sch%C3%BCler-der-Mokganedi-Tlhabanello-High-
School-und-der-Freien-Montessorischule-Landau-zu-Gast-
im-Rathaus (Access 1.11.2024)

43 Lokale Agenda 21 e.V. (2023). Stimmen zur Klimakrise.
Available at: https://la21-trier.de/eine-welt-promotorin-fuer-
umwelt-und-entwicklung/klimakrise/ (Access 20.7.2024)

All information without guarantee.

Suni e.V. bears sole responsibility for the content of the publication; items listed here do not reflect the point of view of Engagement Global gGmbH or the German Federal Ministry for Economic Cooperation and Development or any other sponsor of the described project.

The project was financed by the African-German Youth Office with Engagement Global gGmbH on behalf of the German Federal Ministry for Economic Cooperation and Development within the frame of Teams up! program.

supported by

With funding from the

The exchange was additionally sponsored by the Directorate of Education at Omaheke Regional Council, the Dr. Buhmann Stiftung, the Entwicklungspolitisches Landesnetzwerk Rheinland-Pfalz e.V., the German-Namibian Society, the Katholischer Fonds, the Light for the Children Foundation, Sparkasse Trier and by Suni e.V.
The project was supported by the Office of the Governeur at Omaheke Region, THE BLUE MIND e.V. and by Trier University.
This publication was supported and financed by Suni e.V.